Agroterrorism: Threats and Preparedness

Summary

The potential of terrorist attacks against agricultural targets (agroterrorism) is increasingly recognized as a national security threat, especially after the events of September 11, 2001. Agroterrorism is a subset of bioterrorism, and is defined as the deliberate introduction of an animal or plant disease with the goal of generating fear, causing economic losses, and/or undermining stability. Attacks against agriculture are not new, and have been conducted or considered by both nation-states and substate organizations throughout history.

The results of an agroterrorist attack may include major economic crises in the agricultural and food industries, loss of confidence in government, and possibly human casualties. Humans could be at risk in terms of food safety or public health, especially if the chosen disease is transmissible to humans (zoonotic). Public opinion may be particularly sensitive to a deliberate outbreak of disease affecting the food supply. Public confidence in government could be eroded if authorities appear unable to prevent such an attack or to protect the population's food supply.

Agriculture has several characteristics that pose unique problems for managing the threat. Agricultural production is geographically disbursed in unsecured environments. Livestock are frequently concentrated in confined locations, and then transported and commingled with other herds. Pest and disease outbreaks can quickly halt economically important exports. Many veterinarians lack experience with foreign animal diseases that are resilient and endemic in foreign countries.

Agriculture and food production generally have received less attention in counter-terrorism and homeland security efforts. But more recently, agriculture has garnered more attention in the expanding field of terrorism studies. Laboratory and response systems are being upgraded to address the reality of agroterrorism.

Congress has held hearings on agroterrorism and enacted laws and appropriations with agroterrorism-related provisions. The executive branch has responded by implementing the new laws, issuing several presidential directives, and creating liaison and coordination offices. The Government Accountability Office (GAO) has studied several issues related to agroterrorism.

Appropriations and user fees for USDA homeland security activities have about doubled from a $156 million "pre-September 11" baseline in FY2002 to $325 million in FY2004. Two supplemental appropriations acts added nearly $110 million in both FY2002 and FY2003. For FY2005, the department requested $651 million in appropriations and user fees, but only certain agroterrorism-related items were specifically mentioned in committee reports. The President's budget proposal for FY2006 will summarize the enacted FY2005 homeland security funding for USDA.

In addition to appropriations activity, bills addressing agroterrorism preparedness and coordination among agencies are likely to be introduced in the 109th Congress. A GAO report on coordination between USDA and DHS is expected by March 1, 2005. This report will be updated as events warrant.

Contents

Agriculture as a Target 1
    Overview of the Threat 1
    Importance of Agriculture in the United States 3
    A Brief History of Agricultural Bioweapons 5
    Economic Consequences 6

Federal Recognition of Agroterrorism Threats 8
    Congressional Hearings and Laws 9
        Bioterrorism Preparedness Act 10
        Homeland Security Act 12
        GAO Studies 14
    Executive Branch Actions 15
        HSPD-7 (Protecting Critical Infrastructure) 15
        HSPD-9 (Defending Agriculture and Food) 16
    Federal Appropriations 17
        By Year and Source 18
        By Agency 19
        By Function 21
        Chronology of Appropriations Since September 11, 2001 22

Possible Pathogens in an Agroterrorist Attack 24
    Animal Pathogens 25
        OIE List 25
        Select Agents List 25
    Plant Pathogens 27

Countering the Threat 28
    Deterrence and Prevention 29
    Detection and Response 30
        Laboratories and Research 33
        Federal Authorities 34
    Recovery and Management 35

Issues for Congress 36
    Federal Appropriations 36
    Preparedness 38
    Interagency Coordination 39

Bibliography 41

List of Figures

Figure 1. Geographic Concentration of Agricultural Production 4
Figure 2. USDA Homeland Security Funding, by Year and Source 18
Figure 3. USDA Homeland Security Funding, by Agency 21

List of Tables

Table 1. USDA Homeland Security Funding, by Agency 20

Table 2. USDA Homeland Security Funding, by Function 22

Table 3. Livestock Diseases in the Select Agent List 26

Table 4. Plant Diseases in the Select Agent List 28

Table 5. USDA Food and Agriculture Defense Initiative, FY2005 37

Appendix A. USDA Homeland Security Funding, by Program 46

Agroterrorism: Threats and Preparedness

Agriculture as a Target

Overview of the Threat

The potential of terrorist attacks against agricultural targets (agroterrorism) is increasingly recognized as a national security threat, especially after the events of September 11, 2001. In this context, agroterrorism is defined as the deliberate introduction of an animal or plant disease with the goal of generating fear, causing economic losses, and/or undermining stability.

Agroterrorism is a subset of the more general issues of terrorism and bioterrorism. People more generally associate bioterrorism with outbreaks of human illness (such as from anthrax or smallpox), rather than diseases first affecting animals or plants. Agriculture has several characteristics that pose unique problems for managing the threat:

- Agricultural production is geographically disbursed in unsecured environments (e.g., open fields and pastures throughout the countryside). While some livestock are housed in secure facilities, agriculture in general requires large expanses of land that are difficult to secure from intruders.

- Livestock are frequently concentrated in confined locations (e.g., feedlots with thousands of cattle in open-air pens, farms with tens of thousands of pigs, or barns with hundreds of thousands of poultry). Concentration in slaughter, processing, and distribution also makes large scale contamination more likely.

- Live animals, grain, and processed food products are routinely transported and commingled in the production and processing system. These factors circumvent natural barriers that could slow pathogenic dissemination.

- The presence (or rumor) of certain pests or diseases in a country can quickly stop all exports of a commodity, and can take months or years to resume.

- The past success of keeping many diseases out of the U.S. means that many veterinarians and scientists lack direct experience with foreign diseases. This may delay recognition of symptoms in case of an outbreak.

- The number of lethal and contagious biological agents is greater for plants and animals than for humans. Most of these diseases are environmentally resilient, endemic in foreign countries, and not harmful to humans — making it easier for terrorists to acquire, handle, and deploy the pathogens.

Thus, the general susceptibility of the agriculture and food industry to bioterrorism is difficult to address in a systematic way due to the highly dispersed, yet concentrated nature of the industry and the inherent biology of growing plants and raising animals.

The results of an agroterrorist attack may include major economic crises in the agricultural and food industries, loss of confidence in government, and possibly human casualties. Humans could be at risk in terms of food safety or public health, especially if the chosen disease is transmissible to humans (zoonotic). But an agroterrorist attack need not cause human casualties for it to be effective or to cause large scale economic consequences.

The production agriculture sector would suffer economically in terms of plant and animal health, and the supply of food and fiber may be reduced, especially in certain regions. The demand for certain types of food may decline based on which products are targeted in the attack (e.g., dairy, beef, pork, poultry, grains, fruit, or vegetables), while demand for other types of food may rise due to food substitutions.

An agroterrorism event would cause economic losses to individuals, businesses, and governments through costs to contain and eradicate the disease, and to dispose of contaminated products. Economic losses would accumulate throughout the farm-to-table continuum as the supply chain is disrupted, especially if domestic markets for food become unstable or if trade sanctions are imposed by other countries on U.S. exports. The economic impact can spread to farmers, input suppliers, food processors, transportation, retailers, and food service providers.

Public opinion may be particularly sensitive to a deliberate outbreak of disease affecting the food supply. Public confidence in government could be eroded if authorities appear unable to prevent such an attack or to protect the population's food supply. As the United States evolved away from an agrarian society during the 20th century, food and the fear of inadequate food supplies moved further from the minds of most U.S. residents. However, because food remains an important part of everyone's daily routine and survival, significant threats to the currently-held notion of food security in the U.S. could cause a reordering of people's priorities.

Because an agroterrorist attack may not necessarily cause human casualties, be immediately detected, or have the "shock factor" of an attack against the more visible public infrastructure or human populations, agriculture may not be a terrorist's first choice of targets. Nonetheless, some types of agroterrorism could be relatively easily achieved and have significant economic impacts. Thus, the possibilities are treated seriously, especially in the post-September 11 world.

This report addresses the use of biological weapons against agriculture, rather than the threat of terrorists using agricultural inputs for other purposes.[1] It also focuses more on agricultural production than food processing and distribution.

For more information on the security of the food distribution system, see CRS Report RL31853, *Food Safety Issues in the 108th Congress*, by Donna Vogt.

For more information on chemical and biological weapons in general, see CRS Report RL32391, *Small-Scale Terrorist Attacks Using Chemical and Biological Agents: An Assessment Framework and Preliminary Comparisons*, by Dana Shea and Frank Gottron; and CRS Report RL31669, *Terrorism: Background on Chemical, Biological, and Toxin Weapons and Options for Lessening Their Impact*, by Dana Shea.

Importance of Agriculture in the United States

Agriculture and the food industry are very important to the social, economic, and arguably, the political stability of the United States. Although farming employs less than 2% of the of the country's workforce, 16% of the workforce is involved in the food and fiber sector, ranging from farmers and input suppliers, to processors, shippers, grocers, and restauranteurs. In 2002, the food and fiber sector contributed $1.2 trillion, or 11% to the gross domestic product (GDP), even though the farm sector itself contributed less than 1%.[2] Gross farm sales exceeded $200 billion, and are relatively concentrated throughout the Midwest, parts of the East Coast, and California (**Figure 1**). Production is split nearly evenly between crops and livestock.

Agriculture in the U.S. highly advanced and productive. This productivity allows Americans to spend less than 11% of their disposable income on food, compared with a global average of 20-30%.[3]

Although the number of farms in the 2002 Census of Agriculture totaled 2.1 million, 75% of the value of production occurs on just 6.7%, or 143,500, of these farms. This subset of farms has average sales of $1 million annually, and averages 2,000 acres in size.

The U.S. produces and exports a large share the world's grain. In 2002, the U.S. exported $53 billion of agricultural products (8% of all U.S. exports), and imported $42 billion of agricultural products (4% of all U.S. imports), making agriculture a positive contributor to the balance of trade. The U.S. share of world

---

[1] An example of concern over the misuse of agricultural inputs is the Department of Transportation's regulation (49 CFR Part 172, Subpart I) on securing dangerous agricultural materials such as fuels, chemicals, and fertilizers against theft; see [http://hazmat.dot.gov/pubtrain/AgSecPlan.pdf].

[2] USDA Economic Research Service, *Agricultural Outlook* tables, May 2004, at [http://www.ers.usda.gov/publications/Agoutlook/AOTables].

[3] Henry S. Parker, *Agricultural Bioterrorism: A Federal Strategy to Meet the Threat*, McNair Paper 65, National Defense University, March 2002, at [http://www.ndu.edu/inss/McNair/mcnair65/McN_65.pdf].

production was 39% for corn, 38% for soybeans, and 8% for wheat. The U.S. accounted for 23% of global wheat exports, 54% of corn exports and 43% of soybean exports.[4] If export markets were to decline following an agroterrorism event, U.S. markets could be severely disrupted since 22% of U.S. agricultural production is exported (10% of livestock, and 23% of crops).

Figure 1. Geographic Concentration of Agricultural Production

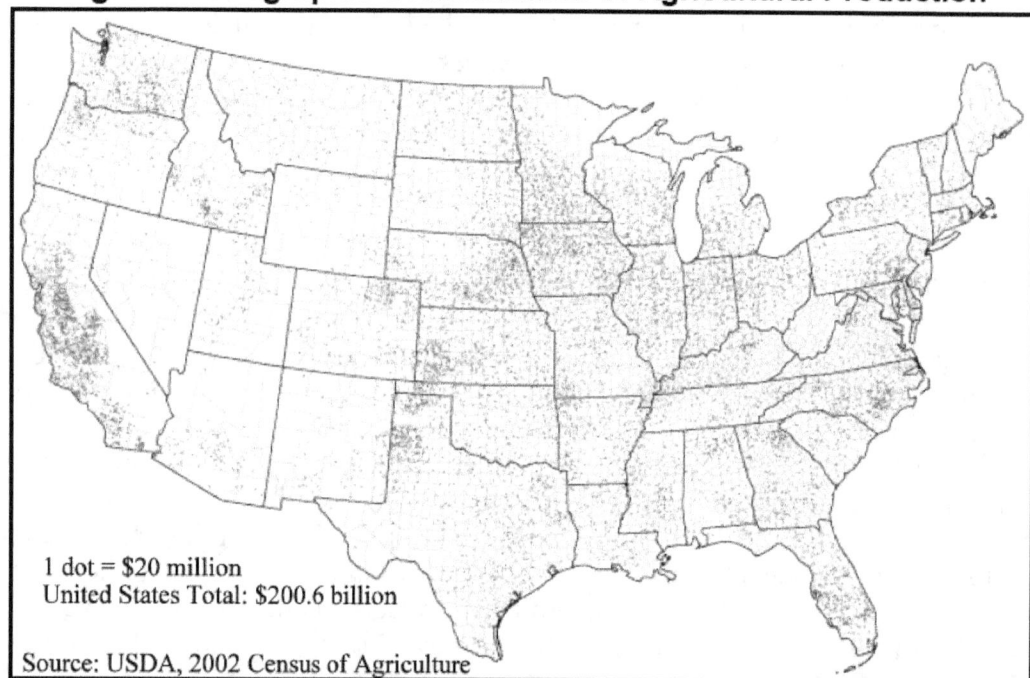

1 dot = $20 million
United States Total: $200.6 billion

Source: USDA, 2002 Census of Agriculture

The price of land is directly correlated to the productivity and marketability of agricultural products, along with federal farm income support payments. In 2002, farm assets exceeded $1.3 trillion, with $1.1 trillion in equity. Land and other real estate accounts for 80% of those assets. Of the 938 million acres of farm land in the U.S., 46% are in crop land, 42% are pasture and range land, and 8% are wood land.[5]

Livestock and poultry are concentrated in various regions of the country, and in large numbers. In 2002, the inventory included 95 million cattle and calves, 60 million hogs and pigs. Farm sales of broilers and other meat-type chickens exceeded 8.5 billion birds.[6]

Cattle are the most widely distributed given the prevalence of small cow-calf herds throughout the country and pockets of dairy on the West Coast, upper Midwest, and Northeast. However, beef cattle feedlots are particularly concentrated from northern Texas through Kansas, Nebraska, eastern Colorado, and western Iowa.

---

[4] U.S. Census Bureau, *Statistical Abstract of the United States: 2003 — Agriculture*, at [http://www.census.gov/prod/www/statistical-abstract-03.html].

[5] USDA Economic Research Service, *Agricultural Outlook* tables, May 2004.

[6] USDA National Agricultural Statistics Service, *2002 Census of Agriculture*, June 2004, at [http://www.nass.usda.gov/census].

Hog inventories are concentrated in the Midwest, especially Iowa and southern Minnesota, and in North Carolina. The production of broilers for poultry meat is concentrated throughout the Southeast, ranging from the Oklahoma-Arkansas border up to the Delmarva peninsula (Delaware-Maryland-Virginia).

A Brief History of Agricultural Bioweapons

Attacks against agriculture are not new, and have been conducted both by nation-states and by substate organizations throughout history.[7] At least nine countries had documented agricultural bioweapons programs during some part of the 20th century (Canada, France, Germany, Iraq, Japan, South Africa, United Kingdom, United States, and the former USSR). Four other countries are believed to have or have had agricultural bioweapons programs (Egypt, North Korea, Rhodesia, and Syria).[8]

Despite extensive research on the issue, however, biological weapons have been used rarely against crops or livestock, especially by state actors.[9] Thus, in recent decades, using biological weapons against agricultural targets has remained mostly a theoretical consideration. With the ratification of the Biological and Toxin Weapons Convention in 1972, many countries, including the United States, stopped military development of biological weapons and destroyed their stockpiles.

Although individuals or substate groups have used bioweapons against agricultural or food targets, only a few can be considered terrorist in nature. In 1952, the Mau Mau (an insurgent organization in Kenya) killed 33 head of cattle at a mission station using African milk bush (a local plant toxin). In 1984, the Rajneeshee cult spread salmonella in salad bars at Oregon restaurants to influence a local election.[10]

---

[7] This report considers only "modern" instances of directing weapons against agriculture and food. However, such attacks can be cited for centuries prior to 1900, usually on a much smaller scale than generally conceived today. Furthermore, this report focuses primarily on biological weapons (rather than chemical weapons) because biological weapons generally are considered the more potent threat for agroterrorist activity.

[8] Monterey Institute of International Studies, "Agro-terrorism," at [http://cns.miis.edu/research/cbw/agromain.htm]; University of Minnesota Center for Infectious Disease Research and Policy (CIDRAP), "Overview of Agricultural Biosecurity," at [http://www.cidrap.umn.edu/cidrap/content/biosecurity/ag-biosec/biofacts/agbiooview.html]; and Peter Chalk, RAND National Defense Research Institute, "Hitting America's Soft Underbelly: The Potential Threat of Deliberate Biological Attacks Against U.S. Agricultural and Food Industry," 2004, at [http://www.rand.org/publications/MG/MG135/MG135.pdf].

[9] Examples of state actors using biological weapons against agriculture include Germany's use of glanders against Allied horses and mules in World War I, the alleged use of anthrax and rinderpest by Japan in World War II, and the alleged use of glanders by Soviet forces in Afghanistan in the 1980s (Source: Monterey Institute of International Studies; and Center for Infectious Disease Research and Policy).

[10] Peter Chalk (2004), p. 29.

Chemical weapons have been used somewhat more commonly against agricultural targets. During the Vietnam War, the U.S. used agent orange to destroy foliage, affecting some crops. Among possible terrorist events, chemical attacks against agricultural targets include a 1997 attack by Israeli settlers who sprayed pesticides on grapevines in two Palestinian villages, destroying up to 17,000 metric tons of grapes. In 1978, the Arab Revolutionary Council poisoned Israeli oranges with mercury, injuring at least 12 people and reducing orange exports by 40%.[11]

Economic Consequences

Economic losses from an agroterrorist incident could be large and widespread.

- First, losses would include the value of lost production, the cost of destroying diseased or potentially diseased products, and the cost of containment (drugs, diagnostics, pesticides, and veterinary services).

- Second, export markets would be lost as importing countries place restrictions on U.S. products to prevent possibilities of the disease spreading.

- Third, multiplier effects would ripple through the economy due to decreased sales by agriculturally dependent businesses (farm input suppliers, food manufacturing, transportation, retail grocery, and food service) and tourism.

- Fourth, the government could bear significant costs, including eradication and containment costs, and compensation to producers for destroyed animals.

Depending on the erosion of consumer confidence and export sales, market prices of the affected commodities may drop. This would affect producers whose herds or crops were not directly infected, making the event national in scale even if the disease itself were contained to a small region.

For food types or product lines that are not contaminated, however, demand may become stronger, and market prices could rise for those products. Such goods may include substitutes for the food that was the target of the attack (e.g., chicken instead of beef), or product that can be certified not to come from regions affected by the attack (e.g., beef from another region of the country, or imported beef). When Canada announced the discovery of mad cow disease (BSE, or bovine spongiform encephalopathy) in May 2003, farm-level prices of beef in Canada dropped by nearly half, while beef prices in the United States remained very strong at record or near record levels. When a cow with BSE was discovered in the United States in December 2003, U.S. beef prices fell, but less dramatically than in Canada.[12]

---

[11] Center for Infectious Disease Research and Policy (CIDRAP).

[12] CRS Report RS21709, *Mad Cow Disease and U.S. Beef Trade*, by Charles Hanrahan and Geoffrey Becker.

Consumer confidence in government may also be tested depending on the scale of the eradication effort and means of destroying animals or crops. The need to slaughter perhaps hundreds of thousands of cattle (or tens of millions of poultry) could generate public criticism if depopulation methods are considered inhumane or the destruction of carcases is questioned environmentally. Dealing with these concerns can add to the cost for both government and industry.

Depending on the disease and means of transmission, the potential for economic damage depends on a number of factors such as the disease agent, location of the attack, rate of transmission, geographical dispersion, how long it remains undetected, availability of countermeasures or quarantines, and incident response plans. Potential costs are difficult to estimate and can vary widely based on compounding assumptions.

A 1994 study by the United States Department of Agriculture (USDA) on African swine fever suggested that if the disease were to become entrenched in the U.S., the 10-year impact would be at least $5.4 billion.[13] The impact in today's dollars could be much higher. A National Defense University study estimates that a limited outbreak of foot and mouth disease (FMD) on just 10 farms could have a $2 billion financial impact.[14] A study by the USDA Economic Research Service (ERS) outlines the wide-ranging implications of a FMD outbreak in the U.S., assigning probabilities for animal losses but not estimating a dollar loss.[15]

Drawing on the FMD outbreak in the United Kingdom in 2001, Price Waterhouse Coopers estimated that the economic impact was $1,389 to $4,477 for each of the 2.6 million head of livestock (cattle, sheep, and hogs) on which indemnities were paid in the U.K. These impacts exceed the value of the animals because of the number of industries affected by the outbreak, ranging from feed suppliers to tourism. Applying the loss ratios from the U.K. incident to the larger U.S. livestock industry, Price Waterhouse Coopers estimates that 7.5 million animals (5.3 million cattle, 1.4 million hogs, and 800,000 sheep) might be destroyed in a similar outbreak in the United States. The resulting economic impact could range from $10.4 billion to $33.6 billion, using the range of impacts estimated from the U.K.[16]

---

[13] Renlemann and Spinelli, "An Economic Assessment of the Costs and Benefits of African Swine Fever Prevention," *Animal Health Insight*, Spring/Summer 1994.

[14] Henry S. Parker (2002).

[15] Kenneth H. Mathews and Janet Perry, "The Economic Consequences of Bovine Spongiform Encephalopathy and Food and Mouth Disease Outbreaks in the United States," Appendix 6 in *Animal Disease Risk Assessment, Prevention and Control Act of 2001 (P.L. 107-9): Final Report of the P.L. 107-9 Federal Inter-Agency Working Group,* January 2003, at [http://www.aphis.usda.gov/lpa/pubs/pubs/PL107-9_1-03.pdf].

[16] Beth Lautner and Steve Meyer, "U.S. Agriculture in Context: Sector's Importance to the American Economy and Its Role in Global Trade," Conference Proceedings of the [White House] Office of Science and Technology Policy Blue Ribbon Panel on the Threat of Biological Terrorism Directed Against Livestock, Washington, DC, December 8-9, 2003, at [http://www.rand.org/scitech/stpi/Bioagpanel].

However, not all assessments agree that the economic consequences of an agroterrorist attack would be large and widespread. A December 2004 report by the Congressional Budget Office (CBO) concludes that the nation's economic loss "would probably be small, primarily because the food and agriculture industry is well adapted to the prospect of disruptions from weather, pests, and occasional health incidents."[17] The report also suggests that the food industry's experience recalling contaminated lots and the existence of government programs "to sustain the incomes of some agricultural producers" might cause the consequences of an agroterrorist attack to "fall within the realm of industry experience and current public plans for detection and response."[18]

Nonetheless, the continuing efforts by federal agencies, state agencies, and private corporations to prepare for agroterrorism appear to be based on the assumption that an attack could exceed the typical experience with naturally or accidentally occurring outbreaks.

The ability of farm commodity programs to compensate for losses due to agroterrorism is limited. Government income support programs subsidize about 25 agricultural commodities (such as corn, wheat, soybeans, rice, and cotton). These supported commodities represent about one-third of gross farm sales. The list of commodities that normally do not receive direct support includes meats, poultry, fruits, vegetables, nuts, hay, and nursery products. These non-supported commodities account for about two-thirds of gross farm sales.[19] Thus, the food products more vulnerable to attack (meats, fruits, and vegetables) do not have existing federal farm income support programs, nor are there income support programs beyond the farm gate for food processors or retailers. Thus, any federal assistance to producers or processors stemming from an agroterrorist attack would likely come in the form of *ad hoc* disaster assistance. Making disaster payments to producers who do not normally receive government payments is technically more difficult than supplementing regular program payments due to drought or flood.

Federal Recognition of Agroterrorism Threats

References to agroterrorism and/or agricultural bioweapons clearly exist in the government, academia, and the press prior to 2000. For example, the Gilmore Commission, in its first report to Congress in 1999, noted that

"... a biological attack against an agricultural target offers terrorists a virtually risk-free form of assault, which has a high probability of success and which also has the prospect of obtaining political objectives, such as undermining

---

[17] Congressional Budget Office, *Homeland Security and the Private Sector,* December 2004, p. 41, at [http://www.cbo.gov/showdoc.cfm?index=6042&sequence=0&from=7].

[18] Ibid.

[19] For more information on farm commodity programs, see CRS Report RS21999, *Farm Commodity Policy: Programs and Issues for Congress*, by Jim Monke.

confidence in the ability of government or giving the terrorists an improved bargaining position."[20]

However, agriculture and food production generally have received relatively less attention, or sometimes were overlooked, in counter-terrorism and homeland security. After what many observers claim to be a slow start after September 11, 2001, agriculture now is garnering more attention in the expanding field of terrorism studies and policies.

Congress has held hearings on agroterrorism and, while addressing terrorism more broadly, has implemented laws and appropriations with provisions important to agriculture. The Government Accountability Office (GAO) has studied aspects of food safety, border inspections, and physical security with respect to agroterrorism. The executive branch has responded by implementing the new laws, issuing several presidential directives, and creating terrorism and agroterrorism task forces.

In its report, the 9/11 Commission (National Commission on Terrorist Attacks Upon the United States) does not make any direct references to agroterrorism or terrorism on the food supply.[21] However, agriculture obviously would be affected, along with other sectors of the economy, by some of the commission's recommendations regarding coordination of intelligence, information sharing, and first responders. An evaluation of those separate issues, however, is outside the scope of this report.

Congressional Hearings and Laws

On November 19, 2003, the Senate Committee on Governmental Affairs held a hearing titled, "Agroterrorism: The Threat to America's Breadbasket," including witnesses from the Administration, state governments, and a private think tank.[22] This was the first congressional hearing devoted entirely to agroterrorism since October 27, 1999. At that time, the Subcommittee on Emerging Threats of the Senate Committee on Armed Services held a hearing titled, "Agricultural Biological Weapons Threat to the United States."[23] During the four years between these hearings, a few individual panelists at more general hearings on food safety, homeland security, or terrorism discussed agroterrorism in reference to other topics.[24]

---

[20] Advisory Panel to Assess Domestic Response Capabilities for Terrorism Involving Weapons of Mass Destruction (also known as the Gilmore Commission), First Annual Report to the President and Congress: *Assessing the Threat*, December 15, 1999, pp. 12-15, at [http://www.rand.org/nsrd/terrpanel].

[21] National Commission on Terrorist Attacks Upon the United States, *The 9/11 Commission Report*, July 2004, at [http://www.9-11commission.gov/report/911Report.pdf].

[22] S.Hrg. 108-491, at [http://a257.g.akamaitech.net/7/257/2422/15jul20041200/www.access.gpo.gov/congress/senate/pdf/108hrg/91045.pdf].

[23] Statements from the October 27, 1999, hearing are available online at [http://armed-services.senate.gov/hearings/1999/e991027.htm].

[24] For example, testimony by Peter Chalk, RAND, "Terrorism, Infrastructure Protection,

(continued...)

Bioterrorism Preparedness Act. The Public Health Security and Bioterrorism Preparedness and Response Act (P.L.107-188, June 12, 2002) contained several provisions important to agriculture. These provisions accomplish the following:

- Expand Food and Drug Administration (FDA) authority over food manufacturing and imports (particularly in sections 303-307).

- Tighten control of biological agents and toxins ("select agents" as discussed in sections 211-213, the "Agricultural Bioterrorism Protection Act of 2002") through rules issued by the Animal and Plant Health Inspection Service (APHIS) and the Centers for Disease Control and Prevention.

- Authorize expanded agricultural security activities and security upgrades at USDA facilities (sections 331-335).

- Address criminal penalties for terrorism against enterprises raising animals (section 336) and violation of the select agent rules (section 231).

New FDA Rules on Food Processors and Importers. The Bioterrorism Preparedness Act responded to long-standing concerns about whether the Food and Drug Administration (FDA) in the Department of Health and Human Services (HHS) had the authority to assure food safety. FDA was instructed to implement new rules for (1) registration of food processors, (2) prior notice of food imports, (3) administrative detention of imports, and (4) record-keeping.[25]

Proposed rules were issued in the spring 2003 followed by a comment period. On October 10, 2003, FDA published two interim final rules for registration of food facilities and prior notice of imports. Those rules were implemented on December 12, 2003, but FDA allowed flexible enforcement during a transition period. The rule on administrative detention of imports was effective upon enactment, with FDA procedures announced on May 27, 2004. The final rule for record keeping is forthcoming.[26]

Registration of Food Processors. The act required FDA to establish a one-time registration system for any domestic or foreign facility that manufactures, processes, packs, and handles food. All food facilities supplying food for the United

---

[24] (...continued)
and the U.S. Food and Agriculture Sector" at the Senate Governmental Affairs Subcommittee on Oversight of Government Management, Restructuring, and the District of Columbia hearing on "Federal Food Safety and Security," October 10, 2001 [http://www.rand.org/publications/CT/CT184/CT184.pdf].

[25] For greater detail about these rules, please see CRS Report RL31853, *Food Safety Issues in the 108th Congress*, by Donna Vogt.

[26] FDA, "The Bioterrorism Act of 2002: Plans for Implementing the Act," at [http://www.fda.gov/oc/bioterrorism/bioact.html].

States were required to register with the FDA by December 12, 2003. Registering involved providing information about the food products (brand names and general food categories), facility addresses, and contact information. Restaurants, certain retail stores, farms, non-profit food and feeding establishments, fishing vessels, and trucks and other motor carriers were exempt from registration requirements. However, many farms had a difficult time determining whether they needed to register based on the amount of handling or processing they performed.

Registration documents are protected from public disclosure under the Freedom of Information Act (FOIA). The registry provides, for the first time, a complete list of companies subject to FDA authority, and will enhance the agency's capability to trace contaminated food. Critics argued that registration created a record keeping burden without proof that facilities will be able to respond in an emergency.

Prior Notice of Imports. As of December 12, 2003, importers are required to give advance notice to FDA prior to importing food. Electronic notice must be provided by the importer within a specified period prior to arrival at the border (within two hours by road, four hours by air or rail, and eight hours by water). With prior notice, FDA can assess whether a shipment meets criteria that can trigger an inspection. If notice is not given, the food will be refused entry and held at the port or in secure storage. Some critics are concerned that the administrative cost of compliance may raise the price of food. Others have argued that perishable imports are subject to increased spoilage if delays arise, or that certain perishables (especially from Mexico) are not harvested or loaded onto trucks before the two-hour notification period. However, implementation of the new system generally has not caused delays and most shippers have been accommodated.

To facilitate compliance, FDA and the Department of Homeland Security (DHS) Bureau of Customs and Border Protection (CBP) integrated their information systems to allow food importers to provide the required information using CBP's existing system for imports. In December 2003, the two agencies agreed to allow CBP officers to inspect imported foods on FDA's behalf, particularly at ports where FDA has no inspectors.

Administrative Detention. Upon enactment of the act, FDA obtained the authority to detain food imports under certain conditions. FDA procedures for making detention were issued on June 4, 2004. To use the authority, the agency must show credible evidence that a shipment presents a serious health threat. Food may be detained for 20 days and up to 30 days, if necessary. The owners must pay the expense of moving any detained food to secure storage. Perishable foods (e.g., fruits, vegetables, and seafood) are to receive expedited review.

Maintenance of Records. FDA published a proposed rule for record-keeping on May 9, 2003, and is still reviewing public comments. In the event of a suspected food safety problem, FDA would have access to records including the facility's immediate supplier, and the immediate customer. Companies could keep the information in any form and use existing records.

The rule would limit access to records that may contain trade secrets and prevent disclosure of such confidential information if records are reviewed. FDA is allowed to reduce the record-keeping requirements for small businesses and to exempt farms, restaurants, and fishing vessels not engaged in processing.

Security for Biological Agents and Toxins. In December 2002, the USDA Animal and Plant Health Inspection Service (APHIS) issued regulations to reduce the threat that certain biological agents and toxins could be used in domestic or international terrorism. APHIS determined that the "select agents" on the list have the potential to pose a severe threat to agricultural production or food products.

The select agent regulations (9 CFR 121 for animals, 7 CFR 331 for plants) establish the requirements for possession, use, and transfer of the listed pathogens. The rules affect many research institutions including federal, state, university, and private laboratories, as well as firms that transport such materials. The laboratories have had to assess security vulnerabilities and upgrade physical security, often without additional financial resources. Some have been concerned that certain research programs may be discontinued or avoided because of regulatory difficulties in handling the select agents.

Extensive registration and background checks of both facilities and personnel were to be conducted in 2003. However, due to delays at the FBI in processing security clearance paperwork, provisional registrations were issued to laboratories that had submitted paperwork by established deadlines.

Homeland Security Act. The main purpose of the Homeland Security Act of 2002 (P.L. 107-296, November 25, 2002) was to create the Department of Homeland Security (DHS), primarily by transferring parts or all of many agencies throughout the federal government into the new cabinet-level department. In doing so, the law made two major changes to the facilities and functions of the Department of Agriculture. The Homeland Security Act transferred:

- agricultural border inspections from APHIS to DHS, and
- possession of the Plum Island Animal Disease Center in New York from USDA to DHS.

Agricultural Border Inspections. Section 421 of the Homeland Security Act authorized the transfer of up to 3,200 APHIS border inspection personnel to DHS. As of March 1, 2003, approximately 2,680 APHIS inspectors became employees of DHS in the Bureau of Customs and Border Inspection (CBP). Because of its scientific expertise, USDA retains a significant presence in border inspection, as described below.

Historically, the APHIS Agricultural Quarantine Inspection (AQI) program was considered the most significant and prominent of agricultural and food inspections at the border. Because of this prominence, AQI was one of the many programs selected for inclusion when DHS was created. Some drafts of the bill creating the new department would have transferred all of APHIS (including, for example, animal welfare and disease eradication) to DHS. Concerns from many farm interest groups about the impact this might have on diagnosis and treatment of natural plant and animal diseases prompted a legislative compromise that transferred only the border inspection function and left other activities under USDA.

DHS-CBP personnel now inspect international conveyances and the baggage of passengers for plant, animal, and related products that could harbor pests or disease organisms. They also inspect ship and air cargo, rail and truck freight, and package mail from foreign countries.

Although the border inspection functions were transferred to DHS, the USDA retains a significant presence in border activities. APHIS employees who were not transferred continue to pre-clear certain commodities, inspect all plant propagative materials, and check animals in quarantine. APHIS personnel continue to set agricultural inspection policies to be carried out by DHS border inspectors, and negotiate memoranda of understanding to assure that necessary inspections are conducted. APHIS manages the data collected during the inspections process, and monitors smuggling and trade compliance. USDA is also statutorily charged in section 421 (e)(2)(A) of the act to "supervise" the training of CBP inspectors in consultation with DHS.

This separation of duties is designed to allow for consolidated border inspections for intelligence and security goals, but preserve USDA's expertise and historical mission to set agricultural import policies.

Adding Agricultural Specialists. Under the CBP cross-training initiative in 2003 (also known as "one face at the border"), most CBP inspectors are trained to perform inspections in all three areas of customs, immigration, and agriculture. However, due to criticism from USDA, inspection unions, and the agricultural industry, DHS created another class of inspectors called agricultural specialists. Agricultural specialists will staff, primarily, secondary inspection stations. These specialists will include former APHIS inspectors who decided not to convert to CBP generalist inspectors and new agricultural specialist trainees.

Before DHS was created, APHIS trained its inspectors in a nine-week course that had science prerequisites. The initial DHS cross-training program announced in 2003 had only 12-16 hours for agriculture in a 71-day course covering customs, immigration, and agriculture. With the creation of the agricultural specialist position, DHS created a 43-day training program for agricultural specialists. The course is taught by CBP and APHIS instructors at a USDA training facility in Frederick, Maryland. The first class graduated on July 13, 2004.[27]

Although DHS is training new agricultural specialists, the future size of the agricultural specialist corps is not certain, given the eventual attrition of former APHIS inspectors. Also, details are not available as to how these inspectors will be deployed and how many ports of entry will be staffed with agricultural specialists (compared with the APHIS deployment prior to DHS). Without agricultural specialists, primary agricultural inspections — the first line of defense for agricultural security — may be conducted by cross-trained inspectors with limited agricultural training.

---

[27] Federal Times, "CBP graduates first class of agricultural specialists," July 15, 2004, at [http://federaltimes.com/index.php?S=255479].

Congressional agriculture committees have been concerned about whether enough attention will be devoted to agricultural inspections by DHS, and whether the U.S. will be as safe from the introduction of foreign pests as it was under the previous inspection system. Inspection statistics from the fall of 2003 indicate that 32% fewer insect infestations were found (under DHS) than in the previous year (under APHIS). APHIS officials cite unfilled agricultural inspector positions and difficulty in adequately cross training former customs and immigration officers to conduct agricultural inspections.[28]

For more information about inspection statistics and the new border inspection arrangement that combines the previously separate customs, immigration, and agriculture inspections, please see CRS Report RL32399, *Border Security: Inspections Practices, Policies, and Issues.*

Plum Island Animal Disease Center. Section 310 of the Homeland Security Act transferred the Plum Island Animal Disease Center to DHS. Prior to June 1, 2003, Plum Island was a USDA facility jointly operated by APHIS and ARS (Agricultural Research Service). This transfer includes only the property and facilities of Plum Island; both APHIS and ARS personnel continue to perform research and diagnostic work at the facility, but DHS also may conduct other research at the facility as well.

GAO Studies. A new report to Congress is expected from the Government Accountability Office (GAO) by March 1, 2005, on interagency coordination between USDA and DHS to protect U.S. agriculture. In the conference agreement for the FY2005 Consolidated Appropriations Act (P.L. 108-447, H.Rept. 108-792), conferees expressed concern over agricultural border inspections and research at Plum Island following the transfer of these activities in 2003 from USDA to DHS.

> The conferees are aware of ongoing concerns within the agriculture sector that the transfer of these responsibilities [border inspection and research] may shift the focus away from agriculture to other priority areas of DHS (H.Rept. 108-792).

Since 2002, four reports from GAO have found gaps in federal controls for protecting agriculture and the food supply. These findings are summarized in testimony prepared for the Senate hearing on agroterrorism on November 19, 2003.[29]

In the first report, following the European outbreak of foot and mouth disease in 2001, GAO found insufficient guidance for border inspectors and an overwhelming volume of passengers and cargo for inspectors to process.[30]

---

[28] *Chicago Sun Times*, "Short-Staffed Port Inspectors Missing Insect-Infested Food," August 6, 2004, at [http://www.suntimes.com/output/news/cst-nws-port06.html].

[29] GAO, *Bioterrorism: A Threat to Agriculture and the Food Supply*, GAO-04-259T, November 19, 2003.

[30] GAO, *Foot and Mouth Disease: To Protect Livestock, USDA Must Remain Vigilant and Resolve Outstanding Issues*, GAO-02-808, July 26, 2002.

Regarding prevention of BSE ("mad cow disease"), GAO found shortcomings in documentation for imports and enforcement of federal feed ingredient bans.[31]

A GAO study on security improvements at food processing companies found that federal agencies, particularly the Food and Drug Administration (FDA), did not have authority to impose requirements or assess security flaws.[32]

Regarding livestock disease research at USDA's Plum Island lab in New York, GAO found that people without adequate background checks had access to secure areas, and that security personnel on the island had limited authority.[33] In response to GAO's security concerns about Plum Island, DHS announced that armed Federal Protective Service personnel would supplement security on the island beginning in June 2004.

Executive Branch Actions

Shortly after September 11, 2001, USDA created a Homeland Security Staff in the Office of the Secretary to develop a department-wide plan to coordinate agroterrorism preparedness plans among all USDA agencies and offices. Efforts have been focused on three areas: food supply and agricultural production, USDA facilities, and USDA staff and emergency preparedness.[34] The Homeland Security Staff also has become the department's liaison with Congress, the Department of Homeland Security (DHS), and other governmental agencies on terrorism issues.

The White House's National Security Council weapons of mass destruction (WMD) preparedness group, formed by Presidential Decision Directive 62 (PDD-62) in 1998, included agriculture, especially in terms of combating terrorism. Many observers note that, as a latecomer to the national security table, USDA has been invariably overshadowed by other agencies.

HSPD-7 (Protecting Critical Infrastructure). In terms of protecting critical infrastructure, agriculture was added to the list in December 2003 by Homeland Security Presidential Directive 7 (HSPD-7), "Critical Infrastructure Identification, Prioritization, and Protection."[35] This directive replaces the 1998 Presidential Decision Directive 63 (PDD-63) that omitted agriculture and food. Both of these critical infrastructure directives designate the physical systems that are

---

[31] GAO, *Mad Cow Disease: Improvements in the Animal Feed Ban and Other Regulatory Areas Would Strengthen U.S. Prevention Efforts*, GAO-02-183, January 25, 2002.

[32] GAO, *Food-Processing Security: Voluntary Efforts Are Under Way, But Federal Agencies Cannot Fully Assess Their Implementation*, GAO-03-342, February 14, 2003.

[33] GAO, *Combating Bioterrorism: Actions Needed to Improve Security at Plum Island Animal Disease Center*, GAO-03-847, September 19, 2003.

[34] USDA Homeland Security Staff, "Homeland Security Efforts," May 2004, at [http://www.usda.gov/homelandsecurity/factsheet0504.pdf]; and National Research Council, *Countering Agricultural Bioterrorism*, 2003, p. 150.

[35] HSPD-7: [http://www.whitehouse.gov/news/releases/2003/12/20031217-5.html].

vulnerable to terrorist attack and are essential for the minimal operation of the economy and the government.

These directives instruct agencies to develop plans to prepare for and counter the terrorist threat. HSPD-7 mentions the following industries: agriculture and food; banking and finance; transportation (air, sea, and land, including mass transit, rail, and pipelines); energy (electricity, oil, and gas); telecommunications; public health; emergency services; drinking water; and water treatment.

HSPD-9 (Defending Agriculture and Food). More significant recognition came on January 30, 2004, when the White House released Homeland Security Presidential Directive 9 (HSPD-9), "Defense of United States Agriculture and Food."[36] This directive establishes a national policy to protect against terrorist attacks on agriculture and food systems.

HSPD-9 generally instructs the Secretaries of Homeland Security (DHS), Agriculture (USDA), and Health and Human Services (HHS), the Administrator of the Environmental Protection Agency (EPA), the Attorney General, and the Director of Central Intelligence to coordinate their efforts to prepare for, protect against, respond to, and recover from an agroterrorist attack. In some cases, one department is assigned primary responsibility, particularly when the intelligence community is involved. In other cases, only USDA, HHS, and/or EPA are involved regarding industry or scientific expertise.

The directive instructs agencies to develop awareness and warning systems to monitor plant and animal diseases, food quality, and public health through an integrated diagnostic system. Animal and commodity tracking systems are included, as is gathering and analyzing international intelligence. Vulnerability assessments throughout the sector help prioritize mitigation strategies at critical stages of production or processing, including inspection of imported agricultural products.

Response and recovery plans are to be coordinated across the federal, state, and local levels. A National Veterinary Stockpiles (NVS) of vaccine, antiviral, and therapeutic products is to be developed for deployment within 24 hours of an attack. A National Plant Disease Recovery System (NPDRS) is to develop disease and pest resistant varieties within one growing season of an attack in order to resume production of certain crops. The Secretary of Agriculture is to make recommendations for risk management tools to encourage self-protection for agriculture and food enterprises vulnerable to losses from terrorism.

HSPD-9 encourages USDA and HHS to promote higher education programs that specifically address the protection of animal, plant, and public health. It suggests capacity-building grants for universities, and internships, fellowships and post-graduate opportunities. HSPD-9 also formally incorporates USDA and agriculture into the ongoing DHS research program of university-based "centers of excellence."

---

[36] HSPD-9: [http://www.whitehouse.gov/news/releases/2004/02/20040203-2.html].

As a presidential directive, HSPD-9 addresses the internal management of the executive branch and does not create enforceable laws. Moreover, it is subject to change without Congressional consent. While Congress has oversight authority of federal agencies and may ask questions about implementation of the directive, a public law outlining an agroterrorism preparedness plan would establish the statutory parameters for such a plan, and, as a practical matter, might result in enhanced oversight by specifically identifying executive branch entities responsible for carrying out particular components of such a plan.[37]

In implementing HSPD-9, the USDA Homeland Security Staff and other agencies are drawing upon HSPD-5 (regarding the national response plan) and HSPD-8 (regarding preparedness). Implementing many of the HSPD-9 directives depends on the executive branch having sufficient appropriations for those activities.

Federal Appropriations

The President's annual budget request to Congress now includes a cross-cutting budget analysis of homeland security issues, as mandated by the Homeland Security Act of 2002 (P.L.107-296, section 889).[38] In USDA, six agencies and three offices receive (or have requested) funding related to homeland security:

- Agricultural Research Service (ARS)
- Animal and Plant Health Inspection (APHIS)
- Cooperative State Research, Education, and Extension Service (CSREES)
- Food Safety and Inspection Service (FSIS)
- Economic Research Service (ERS)
- Agricultural Marketing Service (AMS)
- Departmental Administration (including Office of the Secretary, Homeland Security Staff (HSS), and Office of Chief Information Officer (OCIO)).

Classifying spending on agroterrorism and homeland security requires judgements about which programs are relevant, especially when some have dual purposes.[39] For example, animal and plant health programs would be needed at some level due to natural and accidental outbreaks, regardless of the need for agroterrorism preparedness. Such capacities are being due to agroterrorism. For budgets, all or part of such dual-use activities may be counted as homeland security spending, especially when those functions are expanded due to agroterrorism concerns.

---

[37] For a related discussion on the role of Congress with respect to executive actions, see CRS Report RS20846, *Executive Orders: Issuance and Revocation.* An example of agroterrorism legislation introduced in the 108th Congress is S. 427 and S. 430.

[38] Budget of the United States Government for FY2005: *Analytical Perspectives*, "Homeland Security Funding Analysis" (Chapter 3), pp. 25-39, at [http://www.gpoaccess.gov/usbudget/fy05/pdf/spec.pdf].

[39] Congressional Budget Office (CBO), *Federal Funding for Homeland Security*, April 30, 2004, at [http://www.cbo.gov/ftpdoc.cfm?index=5414&type=1].

Amounts presented in this section, both before and after the creation of DHS, are adjusted to reflect the transfer of the most of the border inspection function from APHIS to DHS. Thus, for comparability to the most recent year, only activities that remain in USDA are included in the tables and figures, regardless of the time period.

By Year and Source. Prior to September 11, 2001, USDA spent about $60 million (FY2002) in regular annual appropriations to combat terrorism, primarily through border inspections and research.[40] Since then, two supplemental and two regular appropriations acts have provided significant additional funds.

Compared to FY2002, the FY2003 regular annual appropriation allocated to USDA homeland security tripled to $180 million, and remained nearly steady at $190 million into FY2004 (**Figure 2**).

Figure 2. USDA Homeland Security Funding, by Year and Source

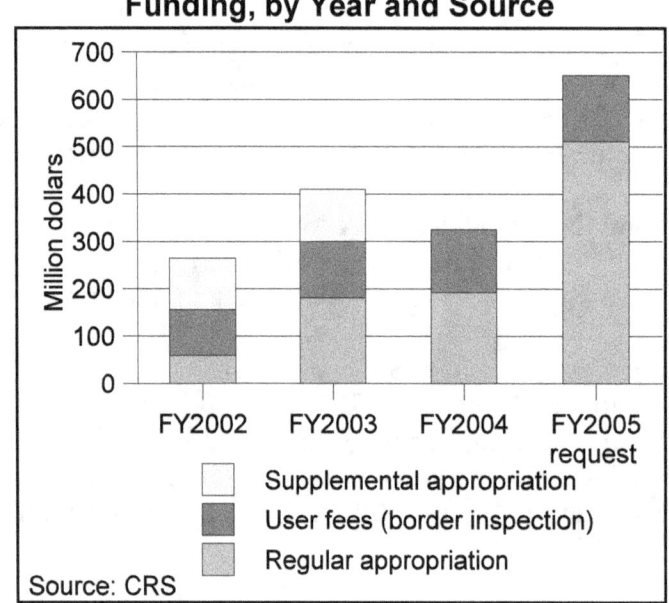

Source: CRS

Two supplemental appropriations (P.L. 107-117 and P.L. 108-11) added nearly $110 million annually in FY2002 and FY2003. User fees for border security contributed between $97 million to $133 million annually from FY2002 to FY2004.

Thus, counting regular appropriations and user fees, USDA homeland security activities have about doubled from a $156 million "pre-September 11" baseline in FY2002 to $325 million in FY2004.

Adding the two supplemental acts to regular appropriations and user fees, USDA homeland security funds total $264 million in FY2002, $410 million in FY2003, $325 million in FY2004 (**Figure 2**).

---

[40] The regular USDA appropriation for FY2002 can be a baseline since it was outlined prior to September 11, 2001, even tough it was enacted two months later.

The President's FY2005 budget also proposed to increase funding to $651 million ($511 million in appropriations and $140 million in user fees). The enacted FY2005 Consolidated Appropriations Act (P.L. 108-447) made some notable increases. However, only certain agroterrorism-related items were specifically mentioned in committee reports, and cross-cutting, comparable figures for FY2005 are not yet available. The President's budget proposal for FY2006 will summarize USDA's enacted FY2005 homeland security funding, and identify funding plans for FY2006.

The FY2005 budget request, and particularly USDA's Food and Agriculture Defense Initiative, is discussed in more detail in the Issues section later in this report.

In addition to these USDA activities, DHS is conducting the agricultural inspections at the border formerly conducted by USDA,[41] and supporting scientific research at universities. These activities are funded both from DHS appropriations and user fees collected by USDA and transferred to DHS. In FY2003, APHIS transferred $69 million of border inspections user fees to DHS, not included in the tables and figures for USDA. In FY2004, APHIS expects to transfer user fees totaling $194 million, and $204 million in FY2005.[42]

By Agency. **Table 1** presents USDA homeland security funding by agency, accounting for user fees and supplemental acts. **Appendix A** contains more detailed information on the programs funded within each agency.

APHIS and ARS have received the vast majority of USDA's $651 million combined FY2002-04 appropriation (excluding user fees) for homeland security. APHIS and ARS have had similar homeland security appropriations ($238 million and $224 million, respectively), but APHIS clearly has more homeland security activity funding if the $349 million of user fees are added to its total for the three years (**Figure 3**).

Most of the APHIS activity in the homeland security area has been for border inspections, predominantly funded through user fees rather than appropriations. Most of ARS's funding has gone for construction of a research and diagnostic laboratory in Ames, Iowa, that ARS operates jointly with APHIS.

---

[41] For more on border security, see the preceding section on the Homeland Security Act.

[42] USDA-APHIS, Explanatory Notes for the President's FY2005 Budget Request, pp. 15-10.

Table 1. USDA Homeland Security Funding, by Agency
(budget authority, $ million)

USDA Agency	FY2002		FY2003		FY2004	FY2005
	Regular P.L. 107-76	Supp. P.L. 107-117	Regular P.L. 108-7	Supp. P.L. 108-11	Regular P.L. 108-199	Request
APHIS* appropriation user fees	19.6 96.5	51.7	77.5 119.0		89.2 133.0	151.9 140.0
ARS	28.0	10.5	44.6	110.0	31.2	227.0
Dept admin	12.0	43.5	18.5		19.3	28.5
CSREES			31.6		38.7	65.8
FSIS		2.6	8.7		12.9	36.5
ERS					1.0	1.0
AMS						0.3
Total	**156.1**	**108.3**	**299.9**	**110.0**	**325.3**	**651.0**
Total yearly	**264.4**		**409.9**		**325.3**	**651.0**
Total, only appropriation	59.6	108.3	180.9	110.0	192.3	511.0
Total, yearly appropriation	167.9		290.9		192.3	511.0

Source: Compiled by CRS from USDA Office of Budget and Policy Analysis spreadsheets, and *Budget of the United States Government for FY2005: Analytical Perspectives*, "Appendix: Homeland Security Mission Funding by Agency and Budget Account," at [http://www.gpoaccess.gov/usbudget/ fy05/pdf/ap_cd_rom/homeland.pdf].

* Includes only the parts of APHIS that remain in USDA after the creation of DHS. Prior to the creation of DHS, USDA was appropriated about $30 million annually (not reflected here) for the border inspection functions transferred to DHS. User fees include only those retained in USDA. In FY2003, APHIS transferred $69 million of user fees to DHS. In FY2004, APHIS expects to transfer $194 million, and $204 million in FY2005.

Figure 3. USDA Homeland Security Funding, by Agency

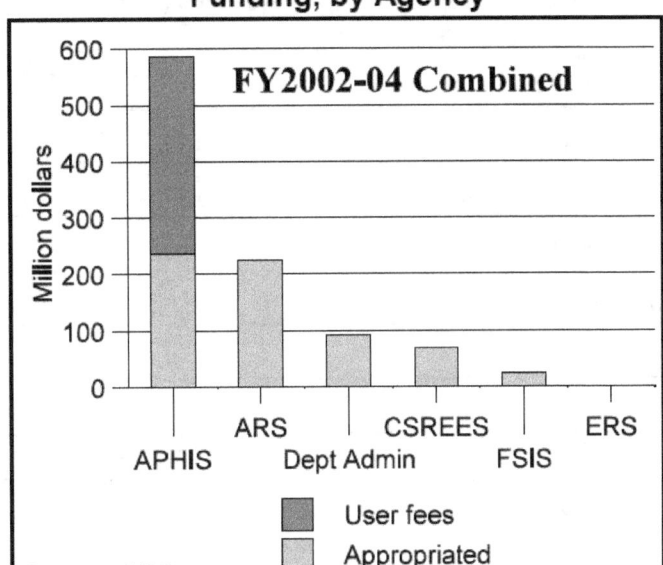

Source: CRS

By Function. For the President's budget request, agencies throughout the federal government categorize their funding based on six mission areas (functions), as defined in the National Strategy for Homeland Security:

- Intelligence and warning
- Border and transportation security
- Domestic counterterrorism
- Protecting critical infrastructure and key assets
- Defending against catastrophic threats
- Emergency preparedness and response

Table 2 presents the information by homeland security function. Over a multi-year period, border inspections are the largest USDA homeland security activity even after most of the inspectors were transferred to DHS. As discussed in the section on the Homeland Security Act, APHIS still inspects passengers and cargo between Hawaii, Puerto Rico and the mainland, and consults on setting inspections policies.

Defending against catastrophic threats is the next largest activity, primarily because of the ARS laboratory construction in Ames, IA. Protecting critical infrastructure has been another large activity, including both physical security improvements throughout USDA and activities for protecting the country's agricultural productive capacity. Such activities include research, diagnostic, and testing programs, and establishing networks and partnerships with States, universities, and other organizations.

Table 2. USDA Homeland Security Funding, by Function
Budget authority, including user fees ($ million)

Homeland Security Mission Area	FY2003	FY2004	FY2005 Request
Border and transportation security*	143.2	163.1	169.3
Defending against catastrophic threats	154.6	20.7	227.0
Protecting critical infrastructure, key assets	60.5	86.3	166.0
Emergency preparedness and response	50.8	54.4	68.7
Intelligence and warning	0.8	0.8	20.0
Total	409.9	325.3	651.0

Source: Compiled by CRS from USDA Office of Budget and Policy Analysis spreadsheets, and *Budget of the United States Government for FY2005: Analytical Perspectives*, "Appendix: Homeland Security Mission Funding by Agency and Budget Account," at [http://www.gpoaccess.gov/usbudget/fy05/pdf/ap_cd_rom/homeland.pdf].

* Includes user fees retained in USDA, but excludes unspecified DHS appropriations for agricultural inspections and user fees collected by APHIS and transferred to DHS. In FY2003, APHIS transferred $69 million of user fees. In FY2004, APHIS expects to transfer $194 million, and $204 million in FY2005. Prior to the creation of DHS, USDA was appropriated about $30 million annually for the border inspections transferred to DHS.

Emergency preparedness and intelligence have received relatively less funding. Primary intelligence gathering is viewed more appropriately as the responsibility of other federal agencies such as the FBI and CIA. These agencies track and act upon bioterrorism information, but USDA needs to be informed also. USDA has limited experience working in the intelligence community, thus building effective partnerships remains a challenge.

Appendix A has more details on these programs by function and agency, and is categorized by homeland security mission area.

Chronology of Appropriations Since September 11, 2001. The following list outlines appropriations acts that have provided funds for homeland security in USDA since September 11, 2001.

- Emergency Supplemental Appropriations for FY2001 (P.L. 107-38; September 18, 2001). Within days of September 11, Congress approved $40 billion in emergency supplemental appropriations partitioned over three time periods. USDA received no money for domestic homeland security programs in the first two installments, but did receive an allocation in the final installment for FY2002 (see FY2002 Emergency Supplemental Act below).

- FY2002 Agriculture Appropriations Act (P.L. 107-76; November 28, 2001). **Table 1** shows that $60 million went to USDA homeland security activities.

- FY2002 Emergency Supplemental Act (P.L. 107-117; January 10, 2002). Congress made the final $20 billion installment from the FY2001 supplemental in Division B of the FY2002 Defense Department Appropriation ("Transfers from the Emergency Response Fund [ERF] Pursuant to P.L. 107-38"). USDA received $328 million for homeland security programs, but, after the creation of DHS, retained functions receiving $108 million.[43]

- FY2002 Supplemental Appropriations Act for Further Recovery (P.L. 107-206; August 2, 2002). In this $28 billion supplemental appropriation, Congress included about $123 million for USDA programs related to homeland security. These amounts, however, were designated among $5.1 billion of "contingent emergency spending" that President Bush chose not to use, and thus the funds were not available to USDA and other departments (see CRS Report RL31406, *Supplemental Appropriations for FY2002*).

- FY2003 Omnibus Appropriations Act (P.L. 108-7; February 20, 2003). **Table 1** show that $181 million went to homeland security activities in USDA.

- FY2003 Emergency Wartime Supplemental Appropriations Act (P.L. 108-11; April 16, 2003). Congress appropriated $110 million to the Agricultural Research Service "for continued modernization of facilities in Ames, Iowa, which will provide a laboratory building, fixed equipment, and associated infrastructure" (H.Rept. 108-076).

- FY2004 Consolidated Appropriations Act (P.L. 108-199; January 23, 2004). **Table 1** shows that $192 million went to homeland security activities in USDA. In this regular appropriations act, conferees made the following statement about USDA's homeland security activities:

"[A]s of September 30, 2003, $80,000,000 remains available to the Department from funds provided through the Emergency Response Fund (ERF) [see discussion of P.L. 107-38 and P.L. 107-117 above], of which nearly $9,000,000 is available to the Secretary. Since these funds were provided, USDA has been one of the slowest Federal agencies to obligate its ERF funds. The conferees are aware of concerns about security, [and] urge the Secretary to act promptly to address identified security needs and to advise the Committees on Appropriations of needs for which additional funds may be necessary" (H.Rept. 108-401).

- FY2005 Consolidated Appropriations Act (P.L. 108-447, December 8, 2004). USDA requested $651 million in homeland security funds

---

[43] This supplemental appropriation precedes the creation of the Department of Homeland Security, and the transfer to DHS of the APHIS border inspection function and the Plum Island Animal Disease Center. Thus, for comparison with more recent figures, a significant portion of the $328 million appropriation did not remain with USDA, as reflected in budget figures provided by USDA for the FY2002 supplemental in Table 1.

for FY2005. The enacted appropriation made some notable increases. However, only certain agroterrorism-related items were specifically mentioned in committee reports, and total USDA homeland security funding has not yet been published. The President's budget proposal for FY2006 will summarize USDA's enacted FY2005 homeland security funding.

Possible Pathogens in an Agroterrorist Attack

Of the hundreds of animal and plant pathogens and pests available to an agroterrorist, perhaps fewer than a couple of dozen represent significant economic threats. Determinants of this level of threat are the agent's contagiousness and potential for rapid spread, and its international status as a "reportable" pest or disease (i.e., subject to international quarantine) under rules of the World Organization for Animal Health (also commonly known as the OIE, the Office International des Epizooties).[44]

A widely accepted view among scientists is that livestock herds are much more susceptible to agroterrorism than crop plants. Much of this has to do with the success of efforts to systematically eliminate animals diseases from U.S. herds, which leaves current herds either unvaccinated or relatively unmonitored for such diseases by farmers and some local veterinarians. Once infected, livestock can often act as the vector for continuing to transmit the disease, facilitating an outbreak's spread, especially when live animals are transported. Certain animal diseases may be more attractive to terrorists because they can be zoonotic, or transmissible to humans.[45]

In contrast, a number of plant pathogens continue to exist in small areas of the U.S. and continue to infect limited areas of plants each year, making outbreaks and control efforts more routine. Moreover, plant pathogens are generally more technically difficult to manipulate. Some plant pathogens may require particular environmental conditions of humidity, temperature, or wind to take hold or spread. Other plant diseases may take a longer time than an animal disease to become established or achieve destruction on the scale that a terrorist may desire.

---

[44] The OIE is an international organization created in 1924 with 166 member countries. It is a well-respected information clearinghouse for animal diseases and health. Member countries report diseases that occur on their territory, and the OIE disseminates the information, allowing other countries to take preventive action. The OIE also analyses scientific information on animal disease control, provides technical support, and develops normative documents that are recognized by the World Trade Organization for international trade and sanitary rules; see [http://www.oie.int].

[45] Some of the biological pathogens of concern to agriculture discussed in CRS Report RL32391, *Small-scale Terrorist Attacks Using Chemical and Biological Agents: An Assessment Framework and Preliminary Comparisons*, by Dana Shea and Frank Gottron.

Animal Pathogens

The Agricultural Bioterrorism Protection Act of 2002 (Subtitle B of P.L. 107-188, the Public Health Security and Bioterrorism Preparedness and Response Act) created the current, official list of animal pathogens that are of greatest concern for agroterrorism. The list is specified in the select agent rules implemented by USDA-APHIS and the Centers for Disease Control and Prevention (CDC) of the Department of Health and Human Services (HHS). The act requires that these lists (**Table 3**) be reviewed at least every two years.

The select agent list for animal pathogens draws heavily from the enduring and highly respected OIE lists of high-concern pathogens. The select agent list is comprised of an APHIS-only list (of concern to animals) and an overlap list of agents selected both by APHIS and CDC (of concern to both animals and humans).[46]

OIE List. Prior to the Agricultural Bioterrorism Protection Act, the commonly accepted animal diseases of concern were all of the OIE's "List A" diseases and some of the "List B" diseases. In 2004, the OIE replaced its Lists A and B with a single list[47] that is more compatible with the Sanitary and Phytosanitary Agreement (SPS) of the World Trade Organization (WTO). The new OIE list classifies diseases equally, giving each the same degree of importance in international trade.[48] Many of these OIE-listed diseases are included in the select agent list (**Table 3**).

The OIE's List A diseases were transmissible animal diseases that had the potential for very serious and rapid spread, irrespective of national borders. List A diseases had serious socioeconomic or public health consequences and were of major importance in international trade. List B diseases were transmissible diseases considered to be of socioeconomic or public health importance within countries and significant in international trade. In creating the new list, OIE reviewed its criteria for including a disease, and the disease or epidemiological events that require member countries to file reports.

Select Agents List. The regulations establishing the select agent list for animals (9 CFR 121.3) set forth the requirements for possession, use and transfer of these biological agents or toxins. They are intended to ensure safe handling and for security to protect the agents from use in domestic or international terrorism. APHIS and CDC determined that the biological agents and toxins on the list have the potential to pose a severe threat to agricultural production or food products.

---

[46] For descriptions of the diseases listed in **Table 3**, see the United States Animal Health Association's "Gray Book," at [http://www.vet.uga.edu/vpp/gray_book/FAD/index.htm], and the OIE's "Technical Disease Cards," at [http://www.oie.int/eng/maladies/en_mal.htm]. Overlap diseases and agents are described by the Centers for Disease Control and Prevention (CDC) at [http://www.bt.cdc.gov/agent/agentlist-category.asp].

[47] OIE, *Terrestrial Animal Health Code*, 13th edition, May 2004, at [http://www.oie.int/eng/normes/mcode/en_sommaire.htm].

[48] Bernard Vallat, "The OIE paves the way for a new animal disease notification system," Editorials from the (OIE) Director General, April 2004, at [http://www.oie.int/eng/Edito/en_edito_apr04.htm].

The 23 animal diseases listed exclusively by APHIS in 9 CFR 121.3(d) — the left column of **Table 3** — include 20 of the OIE-listed diseases and three other disease agents (Akabane, Camel pox, and Menangle) considered to be emerging animal health risks for terrorism. The much larger OIE list includes other diseases that are not listed as "select agents." However, the select agent list was created to account for the additional risks perceived to be posed by terrorism.

The 21 diseases and overlap agents/toxins included by both APHIS and CDC in 9 CFR 121.3(b) — the right column of **Table 3** — pose a risk to both human and animal health. In June 2002, CDC convened an interagency working group to review the list of select agents and develop recommendations regarding possible changes.

Table 3. Livestock Diseases in the Select Agent List

Animal diseases and agents/toxins listed exclusively by APHIS 9 CFR 121.3(d)	OIE class	Overlap diseases and agents/toxins listed by both APHIS and CDC 9 CFR 121.3(b)	OIE class
African horse sickness	E	Anthrax (*Bacillus anthracis*)	M
African swine fever	S	Botulinum neurotoxins	
Akabane		Botulinum neurotoxin-producing species of *Clostridium*	
Avian influenza (highly pathogenic)	A		
Bluetongue (exotic)	M	Brucellosis of cattle (*Brucella abortus*)	B
Bovine spongiform encephalopathy	B	Brucellosis of sheep (*Brucella melitensis*)	C
Camel pox		Brucellosis of swine (*Brucella suis*)	S
Classical swine fever	S	Glanders (*Burkholderia mallei*)	E
Contagious caprine pleuropneumonia	C	Melioidosis (*Burkholderia pseudomallei*)	
Contagious bovine pleuropneumonia	B	Botulism (*Clostridium botulinum*)	
Foot-and-mouth disease (FMD)	M	*Clostridium perfringens* epsilon toxin	
Goat pox	C	(Valley fever) *Coccidioides immitis*	
Heartwater (*Cowdria ruminantium*)	M	Q fever (*Coxiella burnetii*)	M
Japanese encephalitis	E	Eastern equine encephalitis	E
Lumpy skin disease	M	Tularemia (*Francisella tularensis*)	L
Malignant catarrhal fever	B	Hendra virus (of horses)	
Menangle virus		Nipah virus (of pigs)	
Newcastle disease (exotic)	A	Rift Valley fever	M
Peste des petits ruminants	C	Shigatoxin	
Rinderpest	B	Staphylococcal enterotoxins	
Sheep pox	C	T-2 toxin	
Swine vesicular disease	S	Venezuelan equine encephalitis	E
Vesicular stomatitis	M		

Source: 9 CFR 121.3(b) and (d), supplemented with common disease names as appropriate. OIE classes include diseases affecting multiple species (M), cattle/bovine (B), sheep and goats/caprine (C), horses/equine (E), pigs/swine (S), birds/avain (A), and rabbits/lagomorphs (L).

The overlap list includes ten OIE-listed diseases, including anthrax, brucellosis of cattle, brucellosis of sheep, brucellosis of swine, glanders, Rift Valley fever, Q fever, Eastern equine encephalitis, tularemia, and Venezuelan equine encephalitis.

Analysis. It is important to note that the select agent list designates and regulates pathogens, not diseases. Thus, the overlap list between APHIS and CDC is somewhat more comprehensive than a disease-only list, particularly because certain pathogens may not cause a disease, *per se*, but may cause symptoms such as food poisoning or central nervous systems responses.

Some of the pathogens in the select agent list receive more attention than others in discussions about agroterrorism. One reason is that the select agent list was designed to regulate access to and handling of high-consequence pathogens, not the diseases directly.

For example, the causative agent of bovine spongiform encephalopathy (BSE, or "mad cow disease") is considered dangerous enough to be a select agent, even though mad cow disease is less likely to be a terrorist's choice than other diseases. With BSE, infection is not certain, symptoms take years to manifest, and the disease may not be detected — all making credit for an attack more doubtful.

On the other hand, foot and mouth disease (FMD) is probably the most frequently mentioned disease when agroterrorism is discussed, due to its ease of use, ability to spread rapidly, and potential for great economic damage. In testimony before the Senate Governmental Affairs Committee on November 19, 2003, Dr. Thomas McGinn of the North Carolina Department of Agriculture described a simulation of an FMD attack by a terrorist at a single location. Only after the 5th day of the attack would the disease be detected, by which time it may have spread to 23 states. By the 8th day, 23 million animals may need to be destroyed in 29 states.[49]

Widespread animal diseases like brucellosis, influenza, or tuberculosis receive relatively less attention than FMD, hog cholera, or Newcastle disease. However, emerging diseases such as Nipah virus, Hendra virus, and the H5N1 strain of avian influenza (zoonotic diseases that have infected people, mostly in Asia) can be lethal since vaccines are elusive or have not been developed.

Plant Pathogens

The Agricultural Bioterrorism Protection Act of 2002 (Subtitle B of P.L. 107-188) also instructed APHIS and CDC to create the current official list of potential plant pathogens. The Federal government lists biological agents and toxins for plants in 7 CFR 331.3 (**Table 4**). The act requires that these lists be reviewed at least every two years, and revised as necessary.

---

[49] S.Hrg. 108-491, *Agroterrorism: The Threat to America's Breadbasket*, Senate Committee on Governmental Affairs, November 19, 2003, pp. 10, 65, at [http://frwebgate.access.gpo.gov/cgi-bin/useftp.cgi?IPaddress=162.140.64.128&filename=91045.pdf&directory=/disk 5/wais/data/108_senate_hearings].

Table 4. Plant Diseases in the Select Agent List

Plant diseases caused by...	the select agents listed in 7 CFR 331.3
Citrus greening	*Liberobacter africanus, L. asiaticus*
Philippine downy mildew (of corn)	*Peronosclerospora philippinensis*
Soybean rust	*Phakopsora pachyrhizi*
Plum pox (of stone fruits)	Plum pox potyvirus
Bacterial wilt, brown rot (of potato)	*Ralstonia solanacearum*, race 3, biovar 2
Brown stripe downy mildew (of corn)	*Sclerophthora rayssiae* var. *zeae*
Potato wart or potato canker	*Synchytrium endobioticum*
Bacterial leaf streak (of rice)	*Xanthomonas oryzae* pv. *oryzicola*
Citrus variegated chlorosis	*Xylella fastidiosa*

Source: 7 CFR 331.3(a), supplemented with common disease names as appropriate.

Prior to the act, there was not a commonly recognized list of the most dangerous plant pathogens, although several diseases were usually mentioned and are now included in the APHIS select agent list.

The list of nine biological agents and toxins in 7 CFR 331.3 was compiled by the Plant Protection and Quarantine (PPQ) program in APHIS, in consultation with USDA's Agricultural Research Service; Forest Service; Cooperative State Research, Education, and Extension Service; and the American Phytopathological Society. The listed agents and toxins are viruses, bacteria, or fungi that can pose a severe threat to a number of important crops, including potatoes, rice, soybeans, corn, citrus, and stone fruit. Because the pathogens can cause widespread crop losses and economic damage, they could potentially be used by terrorists.

Other plant pathogens not included in the select agent list possibly could be used against certain crops or geographic regions. Examples include Karnal bunt and citrus canker, which both currently exist in the U.S. in regions quarantined or under surveillance by USDA. As with other agents, the effectiveness of an attack to spread such a disease may be dependent on environmental conditions and difficult to achieve.

Countering the Threat

The goal of the U.S. animal and plant health safeguarding system is to prevent the introduction and establishment of exotic pests and diseases, to mitigate their effects when present, and to eradicate them when feasible. In the past, introductions of pests and pathogens were presumed to be unintentional and occurred through natural migration across borders or accidental movement by international commerce (passengers, conveyance, or cargo). However, a system designed for accidental or natural outbreaks is not sufficient for defending against intentional attack.

Consequently, the U.S. system is being upgraded to address the reality of agroterrorism.

The National Research Council outlines a three-pronged strategy for countering the threat of agroterrorism:[50]

- Deterrence and prevention
- Detection and response
- Recovery and management

Even though no foreign terrorist attacks on crops or livestock have occurred in the United States, government agencies and private businesses have not taken the threat lightly. Because of the importance of brand names in marketing, many agribusinesses have prepared response plans or added security measures to protect their product line, looking at threats ranging from the source of their inputs to their retail distribution network. Since the terrorist attacks of 2001, biosecurity is an increasing priority among food manufacturers, merchandisers, retailers, and commercial farmers nationwide.

Deterrence and Prevention

Primary prevention and deterrence interventions for foreign pests and diseases include international treaties and standards (such as the International Plant Protection Convention, and those of the OIE/World Organization for Animal Health), bilateral and multilateral cooperative efforts, off-shore activities in host countries, port-of-entry inspections, quarantine, treatment, and post-import tracking of plants, animals and their products.

Every link in the agricultural production chain is susceptible to attack with a biological weapon. Traditionally the first defense against a foreign animal or plant disease has been to try to keep it out of the country. Agricultural inspectors at pre-clearance inspections and at the U.S. borders are the first line of defense.[51] Smuggling interdiction efforts can act as deterrents before biological agents reach their target.

DHS and USDA already conduct such inspection and quarantine practices, but continued oversight is necessary to determine which preparedness activities and threats need more attention. Off-shore activities include pre-clearance inspection by APHIS of U.S. imports before products leave their port of origin. APHIS has personnel in at least 27 host countries. Although many of these inspections programs were built to target unintentional threats, they are being augmented with personnel and technology to look for intentional threats.

---

[50] National Research Council (2003), p. 41-59.

[51] For more discussion of current border inspections practices and data on past agricultural and other inspections programs, see CRS Report RL32399, *Border Security: Inspections Practices, Policies, and Issues,* by Ruth Wasem et al.

Various U.S. intelligence and law enforcement agencies collect information about biological weapons that could be used against U.S. agriculture. Building and maintaining a climate of information sharing between USDA, DHS, and the intelligence community is necessary, especially so that agriculture is not overlooked compared to other infrastructure and human targets.

Once inside the U.S., many parts of the food production chain may be susceptible to attack with a biological weapon. For example, terrorists may have unmonitored access to geographically remote crop fields and livestock feedlots. Diseases may infect herds more rapidly in modern concentrated confinement livestock operations than in open pastures. An undetected disease may spread rapidly because livestock are transported more frequently and over greater distances between farms, and to processing plants. Processing plants and shipping containers need to be secured and/or tracked to prevent tampering.

An important line of defense is biosecurity, or the use of preventive security measures. On the farm, biosecurity is the use of farm management practices that both protect animals and crops from the introduction of infectious agents and contain a disease to prevent its rapid spread within a herd or to other farms. Biosecurity practices include structural enclosures to limit outside exposure to people and wild animals, and the cleaning and disinfection of people, clothing, vehicles, equipment, and supplies entering the farm.

Most farm specialists agree that livestock farmers are increasingly aware of the importance of biosecurity measures, particularly since the FMD outbreaks in European cattle and the avian flu and exotic Newcastle infections in U.S. poultry. More farm operators are requiring visitors to wear boot covers to guard against bringing in disease. Regardless of the reason for following biosecurity measures (terrorism or accidents), these precautions help prepare farms against agroterrorism.

Detection and Response

In the FY2004 Consolidated Appropriations Act (P.L. 108-199), the conference committee made the following observation about agroterrorism preparedness:

> The conferees agree that emergency preparedness related to field crops, farm animals and food processing and distribution is of critical importance, and that the agriculture and food sectors are part of the critical infrastructure requiring heightened attention and protection. Given the integral roles of state and local governments and the private sector in detecting, deterring and responding to acts of agro-terrorism, the conferees expect the Department of Agriculture and the Department of Homeland Security to coordinate efforts in assisting states, particularly by providing financial and technical support to initiatives oriented toward interstate cooperation in joint preparedness initiatives. The conferees are particularly interested in those states that have developed or are currently developing coordinated interstate initiatives (H.Rept. 108-401, conference report to accompany the Consolidated Appropriations Act of 2004).

Biological attacks on crops and livestock may not be immediately apparent. Therefore, existing frameworks for detecting, identifying, reporting, tracking, and managing natural and accidental disease outbreaks are being applied to combating agroterrorism. Appropriate responses are being developed based on specific pathogens, targets, and other circumstances that may surround an attack.

DHS and USDA have responded with a more detailed and coordinated plan to secure the food supply, particularly with the announcement of HSPD-9. The departments are cooperating on research funding, detection technology, surveillance, partnerships with private industry, and state and local response coordination.[52]

Within private industry, the Food and Agriculture Information Sharing and Analysis Center (ISAC) shares information with government intelligence bureaus through the Department of Homeland Security (DHS). The Food and Agriculture ISAC includes over 40 of the primary trade associations representing food and agriculture. ISAC's exist in several industries and are one of the primary partnerships between government and industry for counter-terrorism cooperation. By combining information among members in the same industry, security problems or attacks may become apparent more quickly than observations within individual companies. In the event of a terrorist incident, the ISAC would facilitate communication within the industry and coordinate response efforts with government officials. The Food and Agriculture ISAC was created in February 2002 and is administered by the Food Marketing Institute. In 2003, three sub-ISAC's were created to cover more specific threats and information sharing for (1) agriculture, (2) food manufacturing and processing, and (3) retail.[53]

In addition to the ISAC, DHS recently created the Food and Agriculture Sector Coordinating Council, which will oversee food security and incident management. The Council includes seven sub-councils: plant producers, animal producers, manufacturers/processors, restaurants/food service, retail, warehousing, and agricultural production inputs.[54]

The exact methods for control and eradication operations are difficult to predict. Past experience and simulations have shown that day-to-day decisions would be made using "decision trees" that include factors such as the geographical spread, rates of infestation, available personnel, public sentiment, and industry cooperation. Response procedures are outlined in the APHIS Plant Protection and Quarantine (PPQ) *Emergency Programs Manual*[55] and the APHIS Veterinary Services (VS) *Federal Emergency Response Plan for an Outbreak of Foot-and-Mouth Disease or Other Highly Contagious Diseases*.[56]

---

[52] DHS Fact Sheet, "Strengthening the Security of Our Nation's Food Supply," July 6, 2004, at [http://www.dhs.gov/dhspublic/interapp/press_release/press_release_0453.xml].

[53] Food Marketing Institute, "Food and Agriculture ISAC (Information Sharing and Analysis Center)," at [http://www.fmi.org/isac/].

[54] Food Chemical News, "Food industry creates new Homeland Security liaison groups," July 12, 2004.

[55] USDA-APHIS Plant Protection and Quarantine (2002), *Emergency Programs Manual*, at [http://www.aphis.usda.gov/ppq/manuals/pdf_files/EPM.pdf].

[56] A summary of the emergency response plan for animals is available from USDA-APHIS

(continued...)

In an outbreak, damage is proportional to the time it takes to first detect the disease. If a foreign disease is introduced, responsibility for recognizing initial symptoms rests with farmers, producers, veterinarians, plant pathologists and entomologists. Cooperative Extension Service agents at state universities are receiving additional training on recognizing the likely symptoms of an agroterrorism attack.

Effective detection depends on a heightened sense of awareness, and on the ability to rapidly determine the level of threat (e.g., developing and deploying rapid disease diagnostic tools). Lessons from disease outbreaks, including the recent FMD outbreaks in Europe and avian flu in Asia and the United States, show that the speed of detection, diagnosis, and control spell the difference between an isolated incident and an economic and public health disaster.[57]

However, in recent years, the number of veterinarians with experience to recognize many foreign animal diseases has declined. This is because the United States has been successful in eradicating many animal diseases. Also, the number of veterinarians available across the country with large animal experience and within APHIS has declined. In light of this trend, APHIS has initiated efforts to increase training for foreign animal diseases and create registries of veterinarians with appropriate experience.

Most of the initial response to the diagnosis of a foreign animal disease is at the state and local level. If an outbreak spreads across state lines or if state and local efforts are unable to control the outbreak, federal involvement quickly follows. Numerous simulation exercises have been conducted by both federal, state and local authorities to test the response and coordination efforts of a agroterrorism attack. Examples of such simulations include the Silent Prairie exercise in Washington (February 11, 2003), the Silent Farmland exercise in North Carolina (August 5, 2003), Exercise High Stakes in Kansas (June 18, 2003).

The last line of defense, and the costliest, is the isolation, control, and eradication of an epidemic. The more geographically widespread a disease outbreak, the costlier and more drastic the control measures become. Officials gained valuable experience from recent agricultural disease outbreaks such as avian influenza in the U.S., Canada, and Asia; FMD in the UK; and citrus canker in Florida. Each one of these epidemics has required the depopulation and destruction of livestock and crops in quarantine areas, indemnity payments to farmers, and immediate suspension of trade.

Of all lines of defense, mass eradication is the most politically sensitive and difficult. Actions taken in each of these outbreaks have met with varying degrees of resistance from groups opposed to mass slaughter of animals, citizens concerned about environmental impacts of destroying carcases, or from farmers who fear the

---

[56] (...continued)
at [http://www.aphis.usda.gov/lpa/pubs/fsheet_faq_notice/fs_ahfmdres.html].

[57] For more information on avian flu and the U.S. response, see CRS Report RS21747, *Avian Influenza: Multiple Strains Cause Different Effects Worldwide*, by Jim Monke.

loss of their livelihood. During the 2001 outbreak of FMD in the United Kingdom, the public was clearly opposed to the large piles of burning carcasses. The disposal of millions of chicken carcasses in British Columbia, Canada, during 2004 also caused a significant public debate. Thus, scientific alternatives are needed for mass slaughter and carcass disposal. Citrus canker eradication efforts in Florida's residential neighborhoods illustrate how science-based measures have been challenged and delayed in the courts, or how farmers may be reluctant to voluntarily test crops or livestock.

Laboratories and Research. Since September 11, 2001, the United States has expanded its agricultural laboratory and diagnostic infrastructure, and created networks to share information and process samples. So far, 19 universities and institutions have been tapped for the USDA-funded National Plant Diagnostic Network (NPDN) and its sister group, the National Animal Health Laboratory Network (NAHLN). A main goal of each is to improve the diagnostic and detection system in the event of a deliberate or accidental disease outbreak.

The effectiveness of these networks will require coordinated outreach, observers say, and cooperative extension services will take on new prominence in their role of providing information about diseases like soybean rust to farmers and others who have regular contact with farms.

Within USDA, several agencies have upgraded their facilities to respond better to the threat of agroterrorism by expanding laboratory capacity and adding physical security. These programs include the ARS research on foreign animal diseases at the Plum Island Animal Disease Center in New York (the physical facility is now managed and operated by DHS) and the ARS Southeast Poultry Research Lab in Athens, Georgia.

Also at USDA, three major laboratories are consolidating operations in a new BSL-3 facility in Ames, Iowa.[58] These include the ARS National Animal Disease Center (NADC), the APHIS National Veterinary Services Laboratories (NVSL), and the APHIS Center for Veterinary Biologics (CVB). The complex will be USDA's largest animal health center for research, diagnosis and product evaluation. The NVSL is especially visible because it makes the final determination of most animal diseases when samples are submitted for testing.

USDA also cooperates with other federal agencies on counter-terrorism research and preparedness, including the ARS and APHIS partnership with the U.S. Army Medical Research Institute for Infectious Diseases at Ft. Dietrick, Maryland. The Ft. Dietrick site offers USDA access to additional high-level biosecurity laboratories. In the recent past, USDA has conducted research on soybean rust at Ft. Dietrick.

---

[58] Biosafety levels (BSLs) are combinations of laboratory facilities, safety equipment, and laboratory practices. The four levels are designated in ascending order, by degree of protection provided to personnel, the environment, and the community; see [http://bmbl.od.nih.gov/sect3tab1.htm]. BSL-1 laboratories handle pathogens of minimal hazard. BSL-4 laboratories handle high-risk, life-threatening diseases with a high risk of aerosol transmission. Only a handful of BSL-4 labs exist in the U.S., including a CDC lab in Athens, Georgia, and an Army lab in Ft. Dietrick, Maryland.

In April 2004, the DHS Science and Technology Directorate announced the department's first university research grants for agriculture as part of its "centers for excellence" program.[59] The University of Minnesota and Texas A&M will share $33 million over three years. Texas A&M's new Center for Foreign Animal and Zoonotic Disease Research will study high consequence animal diseases. The University of Minnesota's new Center for Post-Harvest Food Protection and Defense will establish best practices for the management of and response to food contamination events. Texas A&M is partnering with four universities and will receive $18 million; Minnesota is partnering with ten universities and will receive $15 million.

The House Appropriations Committee addressed agroterrorism research in report language for the FY2004 appropriations bill. The "centers for excellence" program appears to fit the type of research the committee suggested.

> *Agro-terrorism research.* The Committee is familiar with potential agro/bioterrorism vulnerabilities, from animal and plant diseases to food chain introductions. While some agro-terrorism research is already being done by the Department of Agriculture, the Committee is aware of the need for more such research, particularly in the areas of threats to field crops, farm animals, and food in the processing and distribution chain. The Homeland Security Act of 2002 provides for coordination of research between the Department of Homeland Security (DHS) and other relevant federal agencies in various areas of research. Because the Department of Agriculture (USDA) already possesses mechanisms, authorities, and personnel to carry out needed agro/bioterrorism research, the Committee expects to see effective coordination between the USDA and the DHS to move such research forward in an effective and expeditious fashion. The Committee expects USDA to coordinate with DHS to identify research gaps and develop a plan, to include research priorities, for proceeding to fill such gaps. Further, the Committee expects that non-government entities selected to carry out research will be ones with proven expertise in agriculture research, and strong familiarity with USDA animal and plant diagnostic laboratories and practices (H.Rept. 108-193).

Federal Authorities. When a foreign animal disease is discovered, whether accidentally or intentionally introduced, the Secretary of Agriculture has broad authority to eradicate it or prevent it from entering the country.[60] The use of these authorities is fairly common, as shown recently by the import restrictions imposed during the 2004 outbreak of avian influenza in Asia. Federal quarantines and restrictions on interstate movement within the U.S. are also common for certain pest and disease outbreaks, such as for sudden oak death in California and citrus canker in Florida. In addition to federal authorities, most states have similar authorities, at least for quarantine and import restrictions.

---

[59] DHS press release, April 27, 2004, at [http://www.dhs.gov/dhspublic/display?content= 3515].

[60] The Plant Protection Act (P.L. 106-224, Title IV, Sec. 402, June 20, 2000) and the Animal Health Protection Act (P.L. 107-171, Title X, Sec. 10402, May 13, 2002) provide broad regulatory and eradication authorities to the Secretary and to APHIS. These acts replace a patchwork of similar laws dating back many decades by combining authorities into a unified framework.

For example, if an animal disease outbreak is found in the United States, the Secretary of Agriculture is authorized, among other things, to:

- Stop imports of animals and animal products into the U.S. from suspected countries (7 U.S.C. 8303);

- Stop animal exports (7 U.S.C. 8304) and interstate transport of diseased or suspected animals (7 U.S.C. 8305);

- Seize, quarantine, and dispose of infected livestock to prevent dissemination of the disease (7 U.S.C. 8306);

- Compensate owners for the fair market value of animals destroyed by the Secretary's orders (7 U.S.C. 8306(d)); and

- Transfer the necessary funding from USDA's Commodity Credit Corporation (CCC) to cover costs of eradication, quarantine, and compensation programs (7 U.S.C. 8316).[61]

Similar authorities cover plant pests and diseases (7 U.S.C. 7701-7772).

Recovery and Management

Several activities such as confinement and eradication start in the response phase but continue throughout the management and recovery phase. Long-term economic recovery includes resuming the husbandry of animals and plants in the affected areas, introducing new genetic traits that may be necessary in response to the pest or disease, rebuilding confidence in domestic markets, and regaining international market share.

Confidence in food markets, by both domestic and international customers, depends on continuing surveillance after the threat is controlled or eradicated. Communication and education programs would need to inform growers directly affected by the outbreak, and inform consumers abot the source and safety of their food. The social sciences and public health institutions play a complementary role to the agricultural sciences in responding to and recovering from agroterrorism.

If eradication of the pest or disease is not possible, an endemic infestation would result in a lower equilibrium level of production or quality. Resources would be devoted to acquiring plant varieties with resistance characteristics and breeds of animals more suitable to the new environment. This is the goal of the National Plant Disease Recovery System (NPDRS) mentioned in HSPD-9 and being initiated by APHIS.

---

[61] For more information on CCC transfers for plant and animal health programs, see CRS Report RL32504, *Funding Plant and Animal Health Emergencies: Transfers from the Commodity Credit Corporation*, by Jim Monke.

Issues for Congress

Federal Appropriations

The President's budget proposal for FY2006 will summarize USDA's enacted FY2005 homeland security funding, and identify funding plans for FY2006. Because homeland security activities are disbursed throughout USDA and embedded in agency line items, language in appropriations bills or reports is not sufficient to determine the complete spending on agroterrorism.

The enacted FY2005 Consolidated Appropriations Act (P.L. 108-447) made some notable increases over FY2004. However, only certain agroterrorism-related items were specifically mentioned in committee reports. Cross-cutting figures for homeland security spending will become available with background information in the FY2006 budget documents. For FY2005, the President proposed to increase USDA homeland security funding to $651 million ($511 million in appropriations, up 166% from the $192 million appropriated in FY2004, and $140 million in user fees; **Table 1**).

As preliminary background for the FY2006 budget request, USDA's Food and Agriculture Initiative for FY2005 is discussed below. Some of these programs were one-time only expenses (such as construction of the Ames, Iowa, laboratory), while others represented new and continuing programs. Both types are described below.

Within the overall FY2005 request, USDA has highlighted several programs in its newly termed "Food and Agriculture Defense Initiative" (hereafter, the "initiative"). It appears that the preparedness plans outlined in HSPD-9 are coordinated with the initiative, and HSPD-9 could be used to support the request for the initiative in the appropriations process.

The initiative included $381 million (or 75%) of the overall $511 million USDA request for FY2005 homeland security-related activities. Thus, it does not include certain ongoing programs such as border security. The programs that USDA selected for the initiative were funded at $79 million in FY2004, and $204 million in FY2003 (**Table 5**).

The largest item in the initiative is the final appropriation for ARS to complete construction of the Ames, IA, BSL-3 animal research and diagnostic laboratory. The FY2005 request for this laboratory is $178 million, 47% of the Food and Agriculture Defense Initiative, and 35% of the overall USDA homeland security request. P.L. 108-447 funded the Ames construction project at $122 million.

For APHIS, P.L. 108-447 provides $2.0 million for the new bio-surveillance program ($5 million requested). Vaccine banks are funded at $3 million ($6 million requested). Funding for emergency coordinators rises to 4.0 million ($4.6 million requested). State cooperative agreements increase by $3.6 million, select agents by $2.5 million, the national animal laboratory network by $2.9 million. Requested funding of $7.1 million for physical security enhancements throughout APHIS was not included in the final law.

Table 5. USDA Food and Agriculture Defense Initiative, FY2005
(million $)

	Agency	FY2003 Actual	FY2004 Est.	FY2005 Request
Food Defense:		**11**	**15**	**53**
Food Emergency Response Network	FSIS	0	0	14
Surveillance and monitoring	FSIS	1	1	6
FSIS enhanced inspections	FSIS	0	2	2
Lab upgrades, physical security	FSIS	1	3	6
Education, training, other	FSIS	6	6	8
Research	ARS	2	2	16
Agriculture Defense:		**193**	**65**	**328**
Ames , Iowa BSL-3 facility	ARS	143	0	178
Research	ARS	10	12	15
National Plant Disease Recovery	ARS	0	0	6
Regional Diagnostic Network	CSREES	0	8	30
Higher educ. agrosecurity program	CSREES	0	0	5
Plant and animal health monitoring	APHIS	4	4	50
National Veterinary Vaccine Bank	APHIS	0	0	7
Other	APHIS	37	40	38
Total, Food and Agriculture Defense Initiative	**USDA**	**204**	**79**	**381**

Source: USDA Budget Summary, FY2005.

Many of the initiative's programs were designed to improve the Federal government's ability to more quickly identify and characterize an agroterrorist attack through surveillance and monitoring (FY2005 request: $6 million for FSIS, $39 million for APHIS). In its justification for the initiative, USDA said these activities would promote data sharing and joint analysis among federal, state and local levels, and establish a federal multi-agency intelligence capability integrated through DHS.

An example of such coordination is the new Food Emergency Response Network (FERN) of laboratories (a new appropriation request of $14 million for FSIS in FY2005 and $23 million for the Food and Drug Administration, FDA). These computer networks allow labs to improve information sharing, rapid identification, and consistent diagnostic methods for contaminated foods.

Another preparedness effort in the initiative is the National Veterinary Vaccine Bank and the National Plant Disease Recovery System (both of which are mentioned in HSPD-9). These two programs had no budget line in FY2004.

The plant recovery system is a joint effort with the seed industry to develop resistant seed varieties and, in the event of catastrophic disease or pest outbreak, to provide them to producers before the next planting season (a new appropriation request of $6 million in FY2005). The vaccine bank would improve preparedness for bioterrorism against livestock and complement the North American FMD Vaccine Bank. APHIS has a long term plan to stockpile enough vaccine to adequately treat five foreign animal diseases.[62] For FY2005, APHIS requested $6 million of no-year money to be available when viable vaccine choices become available. In the short term, APHIS hopes to obtain enough vaccine for one of these diseases in FY2005.

More details on the FY2005 appropriation will be available after the FY2006 request is released.

Preparedness

Increasing the level of preparedness remains a concern throughout government, not only for agroterrorism, but also for other forms of terrorism. Bills are expected to be introduced in the 109th Congress to authorize funding or otherwise improve the level of preparedness for an agroterrorist attack.

In the 108th Congress, two complementary bills addressing agroterrorism preparedness were introduced: S. 427 (the Agriculture Security Assistance Act) and S. 430 (the Agriculture Security Preparedness Act). S. 427 addressed funding for state and local preparedness, and awareness programs and grants for farmers. S. 430 sought to improve coordination between USDA and other federal agencies. Both bills were introduced in February 2003 and addressed different aspects of agroterrorism preparedness by amending the Homeland Security Act of 2002 (P.L. 107-296). The bills were referred to the Senate Agriculture Committee, which did not act on the bills during the 108th Congress. The bills were sponsored by Senator Akaka of the Homeland Security and Governmental Affairs Committee.

The bills sought to provide more concrete Congressional instructions and budget authorizations for agroterrorism preparedness. However, similar results may occur if the presidential directive HSPD-9 is implemented successfully. The presidential directives facilitating agroterrorism preparedness did not exist when the bills were introduced.

While Congress certainly has oversight authority of federal agencies and may ask questions about implementation of HSPD-9, a public law outlining and directing the implementation of an agroterrorism preparedness plan would establish the statutory parameters for such a plan, and, as a practical matter, might result in enhanced oversight by specifically identifying executive branch entities responsible for carrying out particular components of such a plan.

The Agriculture Security Assistance Act (S. 427, 108th Congress) would have provided funding for state and local vulnerability assessments, plans, and expanded

---

[62] In the past, animal disease outbreaks have been managed by quickly destroying affected herds. However, smaller Federal and state work forces, environmental restrictions, animal welfare concerns, and trade rules may affect feasibility of large-scale culling. For certain species and diseases, vaccines could become as beneficial for controlling the disease, and might be more economical (Explanatory Notes for the FY2005 APHIS budget request).

information systems. The bill would have authorized such sums as necessary for emergency response plans, $2.5 million for geographic information systems, and $5 million for grants to state and local animal health officials.

The bill would also have created awareness programs and grants for farm-level producers to improve biosecurity measures. It contained an authorization of $5 million for the development and dissemination of on-farm biosecurity guidelines, and $5 million for on-farm biosecurity improvement grants (up to $10,000 per farm, and thus reaching at least 500 farms). These first-year authorizations were followed by such sums as necessary for succeeding years. Actual funding would have been determined by appropriations.

Interagency Coordination

Shortly following enactment of the Homeland Security Act and the 2003 transfer from USDA to DHS of agricultural border inspections and the Plum Island agricultural research facility, concerns over DHS dedication to these agricultural functions began rising. Some Members and industry groups worried that DHS would concentrate on more immediate or visible homeland security issues such as immigration, and neglect agricultural functions. Some were also concerned that personnel and resources formerly devoted to agriculture would be shifted to other DHS areas (for more background, see the earlier section on the Homeland Security Act). Concern over coordination and communication between legacy agencies and DHS is not unique to agriculture.

In the conference report for the FY2005 Consolidated Appropriations Act (P.L. 108-447, H.Rept. 108-792), conferees expressed their concern over two agricultural functions transferred to DHS, and requested a GAO study of coordination between DHS and USDA.

> The conferees are aware of ongoing concerns within the agriculture sector that the transfer of these responsibilities [border inspection and research] may shift the focus away from agriculture to other priority areas of DHS. In order to ensure that the interests of U.S. agriculture are protected and that the intent of the Homeland Security Act of 2002 is being fully met, including the proper allocation of AQI [Agricultural Quarantine Inspection] and other funds, the conferees request the Government Accountability Office to provide a report, no later than March 1, 2005, on the coordination between USDA and DHS in protecting the U.S. agriculture sector, including a description of the long-term objectives of joint activities at Plum Island and the effectiveness of AQI and other inspection activities (H.Rept. 108-792).

This GAO report will be watched carefully in the agricultural and appropriations committees. Hearings and further discussion about managing these functions may follow during the 109th Congress.

In the 108th Congress, the Agriculture Security Preparedness Act (S. 430) sought to improve coordination between USDA and other federal agencies. These agencies included the Department of Homeland Security (DHS) and intelligence agencies for tracking targets and incidents, the Federal Emergency Management Agency (FEMA) for disaster plans, the Department of Health and Human Services (HHS) for animal care, and the Department of State for foreign agricultural disease notification and cooperation. The bill would have provided for a USDA review of laboratory capacity, and a Department of Justice review of legal authorities for response plans.

The bill would have created "liaison" positions in DHS, specifically within the Federal Emergency Management Agency (FEMA), and HHS. USDA already has a liaison staff in the Office of the Secretary, namely the Homeland Security Staff. While not the same as proposed in S. 430 (108th Congress), this existing USDA liaison appears to be undertaking a role similar to that proposed by the bill.

Bibliography

American Phytopathological Society. "Crop Biosecurity: Are We Prepared?" White Paper, May 2003, [http://www.apsnet.org/members/ppb/PDFs/CropBiosecurity WhitePaper5-03.pdf].

Applebaum, R. "Terrorism and the Nation's Food Supply," *Journal of Food Science*. Vol. 69, No. 2, March 2004, [http://bookstore.myift.org/orders/iftstore/ift-9984-2238-5934-8765-house/21259jfsv69n2pCRH0047-0054ms20031209.pdf].

Belasco, A., and L. Nowels, *Supplemental Appropriations for FY2002: Combating Terrorism and Other Issues*, CRS Report RL31406, August 30, 2002.

Casagrande, R. "Biological Warfare Targeted at Livestock," *BioScience*, Vol. 52, No. 7 (July 2002), pp. 577-581, [http://www.bioone.org/pdfserv/i0006-3568-052-07-0577.pdf].

Centers for Disease Control and Prevention. *Bioterrorism Agents and Diseases*, [http://www.bt.cdc.gov/agent/agentlist-category.asp].

Chalk, Peter. "Hitting America' Soft Underbelly: The Potential Threat of Deliberate Biological Attacks Against U.S. Agricultural and Food Industry", RAND National Defense Research Institute, January 2004, [http://www.rand.org/publications/MG/MG135/MG135.pdf].

Chalk, Peter. "Terrorism, Infrastructure Protection, and the U.S. Food and Agriculture Sector." Testimony for the Senate Governmental Affairs Subcommittee on Oversight of Government Management, Restructuring, and the District of Columbia hearing on "Federal Food Safety and Security," October 10, 2001, [http://www.rand.org/publications/CT/CT184/CT184.pdf].

Congressional Budget Office. *Federal Terrorism Reinsurance: An Update*, January 2005, [http://www.cbo.gov/ftpdocs/60xx/doc6049/01-05-Terrorism.pdf].

Congressional Budget Office. *Homeland Security and the Private Sector*, December 2004, [http://www.cbo.gov/showdoc.cfm?index=6042&sequence=0&from=7].

Congressional Budget Office. *Federal Funding for Homeland Security*, April 30, 2004, [http://www.cbo.gov/ftpdoc.cfm?index=5414&type=1].

Council of State Governments. *Agricultural Terrorism in the Midwest: Risks, Threats and State Responses*, December 2002, [http://www.csgmidwest.org/MemberServices/Publications/ReportsNewsltrs/AgTerrorism.pdf].

Cupp, O., D. Walker, and J. Hillison. "Agroterrorism in the U.S.: Key Security Challenge for the 21st Century, *Biosecurity and Bioterrorism*, Vol. 2, No. 2, 2004, [http://www.biosecurityjournal.com/PDFs/V2n204/p97.pdf].

Food and Drug Administration, "The Bioterrorism Act of 2002: Plans for Implementing the Act," [http://www.fda.gov/oc/bioterrorism/bioact.html].

Food Chemical News, "Food industry creates new Homeland Security liaison groups," July 12, 2004.

Food Marketing Institute, "Food and Agriculture ISAC (Information Sharing and Analysis Center)," [http://www.fmi.org/isac/].

Gilmore Commission. Advisory Panel to Assess Domestic Response Capabilities for Terrorism Involving Weapons of Mass Destruction (also known as the Gilmore Commission). First Annual Report to the President and Congress: *Assessing the Threat*. December 15, 1999, pp. 12-15, [http://www.rand.org/nsrd/terrpanel].

Government Accountability Office. *Bioterrorism: A Threat to Agriculture and the Food Supply*, GAO-04-259T, November 19, 2003.

Government Accountability Office. *Foot and Mouth Disease: To Protect Livestock, USDA Must Remain Vigilant and Resolve Outstanding Issues*, GAO-02-808, July 26, 2002.

Government Accountability Office. *Mad Cow Disease: Improvements in the Animal Feed Ban and Other Regulatory Areas Would Strengthen U.S. Prevention Efforts*, GAO-02-183, January 25, 2002.

Government Accountability Office. *Food-Processing Security: Voluntary Efforts Are Under Way, But Federal Agencies Cannot Fully Assess Their Implementation*, GAO-03-342, February 14, 2003.

Government Accountability Office. *Combating Bioterrorism: Actions Needed to Improve Security at Plum Island Animal Disease Center*, GAO-03-847, September 19, 2003.

Halstead, T. J. *Executive Orders: Issuance and Revocation*, CRS Report RS20846, March 19, 2001.

Hanrahan, Charles, and Geoffrey Becker. *Mad Cow Disease and U.S. Beef Trade*, CRS Report RS21709, August 4, 2004.

Kohnen, A. "Responding to the Threat of Agroterrorism: Specific Recommendations for the United States Department of Agriculture." BCSIA Discussion Paper 2000-29, John F. Kennedy School of Government, Harvard University, October 2000, [http://bcsia.ksg.harvard.edu/publication.cfm?ctype=paper&item_id=78].

Mathews, Kenneth H., and Janet Perry. "The Economic Consequences of Bovine Spongiform Encephalopathy and Food and Mouth Disease Outbreaks in the United States," Appendix 6 in *Animal Disease Risk Assessment, Prevention and Control Act of 2001 (P.L. 107-9): Final Report of the P.L. 107-9 Federal Inter-Agency Working Group*. January 2003.

Meyerson, L., and J. Reaser. "Biosecurity: Moving Toward a Comprehensive Approach," *BioScience*, Vol. 52, No. 7 (July 2002), pp. 593-600, [http://www.bioone.org/pdfserv/i0006-3568-052-07-0593.pdf].

Monke, Jim. *Avian Influenza: Multiple Strains Cause Different Effects Worldwide*, CRS Report RS21747, May 14, 2004.

Monke, Jim. *Farm Commodity Policy: Programs and Issues for Congress*, CRS Report RS21999, December 8, 2004.

Monke, Jim. *Funding Plant and Animal Health Emergencies: Transfers from the Commodity Credit Corporation*, CRS Report RL32504, July 30, 2004.

Monterey Institute of International Studies, "Agro-terrorism," [http://cns.miis.edu/research/cbw/agromain.htm].

National Commission on Terrorist Attacks Upon the United States. *The 9/11 Commission Report*, July 2004, [http://www.9-11commission.gov/report/911Report.pdf].

National Institutes of Health. *Summary of Recommended Biosafety Levels for Infectious Agents*, [http://bmbl.od.nih.gov/sect3tab1.htm].

National Research Council of the National Academies, *Countering Agricultural Bioterrorism*, 2003, [http://www.nap.edu/catalog/10505.html].

Nipp, Terry. "Agrosecurity: The Role of the Agricultural Experiment Stations," *Journal of Food Science*. Vol. 69, No. 2, March 2004, [http://bookstore.myift.org/orders/iftstore/ift-9984-2238-5934-8765-house/21259jfsv69n2pCRH0047-0054 ms20031209.pdf].

Office International des Epizooties (World Organization for Animal Health) "Technical Disease Cards," [http://www.oie.int/eng/maladies/en_fiches.htm].

Office International des Epizooties (World Organization for Animal Health) *Terrestrial Animal Health Code*, 12th edition, May 2003, [http://www.oie.int/eng/normes/MCode/A_summry.htm].

Parker, Henry S., *Agricultural Bioterrorism: A Federal Strategy to Meet the Threat*, McNair Paper 65, National Defense University, March 2002, [http://www.ndu.edu/inss/McNair/mcnair65/McN_65.pdf].

Pate, J., and G. Cameron. "Covert Biological Weapons Attacks Against Agricultural Targets," BCSIA Discussion Paper 2001-9, John F. Kennedy School of Government, Harvard University, August 2001, [http://bcsia.ksg.harvard.edu/publication.cfm?ctype=paper&item_id=114].

Renlemann and Spinelli, "An Economic Assessment of the Costs and Benefits of African Swine Fever Prevention," *Animal Health Insight*, Spring/Summer 1994.

Rogers, P., S. Whitby, and M. Dando. "Biological Warfare Against Crops," *Scientific American*, June 1999, p. 70-75.

Segarra, Alejandro. *Agroterrorism: Options in Congress*, CRS Report RL31217, July 17, 2002.

Shea, Dana, and Frank Gottron. *Small-scale Terrorist Attacks Using Chemical and Biological Agents: An Assessment Framework and Preliminary Comparisons*, CRS Report RL32391, June 23, 2004.

Shea, Dana. *Terrorism: Background on Chemical, Biological, and Toxin Weapons and Options for Lessening Their Impact*, CRS Report RL31669, December 1, 2004.

University of Minnesota Center for Infectious Disease Research and Policy (CIDRAP)," Overview of Agricultural Biosecurity," [http://www.cidrap.umn.edu/cidrap/content/biosecurity/ag-biosec/biofacts/agbiooview.html].

United States Animal Health Association "Gray Book" [of Animal Diseases], [http://www.vet.uga.edu/vpp/gray_book/FAD/index.htm].

U.S. Census Bureau, *Statistical Abstract of the United States: 2003 — Agriculture*, [http://www.census.gov/prod/www/statistical-abstract-03.html].

USDA Animal and Plant Health Inspection Service. *Explanatory Notes for the President's FY2005 Budget Request.*

USDA Animal and Plant Health Inspection Service, Plant Protection and Quarantine. *Emergency Programs Manual*, 2002, [http://www.aphis.usda.gov/ppq/manuals/pdf_files/EPM.pdf].

USDA Economic Research Service, *Agricultural Outlook* tables, [http://www.ers.usda.gov/publications/Agoutlook/AOTables].

USDA Homeland Security Staff. "Homeland Security Efforts," May 2004, [http://www.usda.gov/homelandsecurity/factsheet0504.pdf].

USDA National Agricultural Statistics Service, *2002 Census of Agriculture*, June 2004, [http://www.nass.usda.gov/census].

U.S. Department of Homeland Security. "Strengthening the Security of Our Nation's Food Supply," DHS Fact Sheet, July 6, 2004, [http://www.dhs.gov/dhspublic/interapp/press_release/press_release_0453.xml].

U.S. Food and Drug Administration, "The Bioterrorism Act of 2002: Plans for Implementing the Act," [http://www.fda.gov/oc/bioterrorism/bioact.html].

U.S. Senate Committee on Governmental Affairs. "Agroterrorism: The Threat to America's Breadbasket," S.Hrg. 108-491, November 19, 2003, [http://a257.g.akamaitech.net/7/257/2422/15jul20041200/www.access.gpo.gov/congress/senate/pdf/108hrg/91045.pdf].

U.S. Senate Committee on Armed Services, Subcommittee on Emerging Threats. "Agricultural Biological Weapons Threat to the United States." Hearing on October 27, 1999, [http://armed-services.senate.gov/hearings/1999/e991027. htm].

Wasem, Lake, Seghetti, Monke, and Vina. *Border Security: Inspections Practices, Policies, and Issues*, CRS Report RL32399, August 2, 2004.

Wheelis, M., R. Casagrande, and L. Madden. "Biological Attack on Agriculture: Low-Tech, High-Impact Bioterrorism," *BioScience*, Vol. 52, No. 7 (July 2002), pp. 569-576, [http://www.bioone.org/pdfserv/i0006-3568-052-07-0569.pdf].

White House. *Budget of the United States Government for FY2005: Analytical Perspectives*, "Homeland Security Funding Analysis" (Chapter 3), pp. 25-39, [http://www.gpoaccess.gov/usbudget/fy05/pdf/spec.pdf].

White House. Homeland Security Presidential Directive 7 (HSPD-7): "Critical Infrastructure Identification, Prioritization, and Protection," [http://www. whitehouse.gov/news/releases/2003/12/20031217-5.html].

White House. Homeland Security Presidential Directive 9 (HSPD-9): "Defense of United States Agriculture and Food," [http://www.whitehouse.gov/news/ releases/2004/02/20040203-2.html].

White House Office of Science and Technology Policy. *Conference Proceedings of the Blue Ribbon Panel on The Threat of Biological Terrorism Directed Against Livestock*, Washington, DC, December 8-9, 2003, [http://www.rand.org/ scitech/stpi/Bioagpanel].

World Health Organization. *Terrorist Threats to Food: Guidance For Establishing And Strengthening Prevention And Response Systems*, 2002, [http://www. who.int/foodsafety/publications/general/en/terrorist.pdf].

Vogt, Donna. *Food Safety Issues in the 108th Congress*, CRS Report RL31853, April 20, 2004.

Zink, D. "Agroterrorism: Issues of Reality," *Journal of Food Science*. Vol. 69, No. 2, March 2004, [http://bookstore.myift.org/orders/iftstore/ift-9984-2238-5934-8765-house/21259jfsv69n2pCRH0047-0054ms20031209.pdf].

Appendix A. USDA Homeland Security Funding, by Program

Homeland Security Mission Area USDA Agency and Program	Budget authority ($ million)		
	FY2003	FY2004	FY2005 Request
Border and transportation security	**143.2**	**163.1**	**169.3**
FSIS: Enhanced inspections		2.0	2.0
APHIS: Ag Quarantine Inspection, approp.	24.2	25.4	21.6
APHIS: Ag Quarantine Inspection, user fees	119.0	133.0	140.0
APHIS: Import/Export		2.7	5.7
Defending against catastrophic threats	**154.6**	**20.7**	**227.0**
ARS: Ames, IA, BSL-3 facility	142.8	0.0	178.0
ARS: Research	11.8	20.7	43.0
ARS: National Plant Recovery System			6.0
Protecting critical infrastructure, key assets	**60.5**	**86.3**	**166.0**
CSREES: Regional Diagnostic Network		7.9	30.0
Dept. Admin.: Physical security	8.0	7.9	13.6
APHIS: Physical security			7.1
ARS: Physical security	0.6	10.5	
FSIS: Physical security	0.2	0.3	0.2
FSIS: Expanded laboratory capabilities	1.0	3.1	3.1
FSIS: Laboratories for chemical, radiological			2.5
Dept. Admin.: Vulnerability assessments	0.1	0.1	0.1
APHIS: Animal health regulatory enforcement		1.0	1.0
APHIS: Select agents - plants			1.5
APHIS: Cooperative ag pest survey agreements			6.1
APHIS: National wildlife surveillance			5.0
APHIS: International information gathering			2.5
APHIS: National animal identification system			4.0
APHIS: Animal health monitoring			2.1
APHIS: Pest detection technology			2.0
APHIS: Foreign animal disease laboratory			2.4
APHIS: National germplasm laboratory			3.0
APHIS: National animal health lab network			1.7
APHIS: Emergency coordination - plants			1.5
APHIS: Emergency coordination - animals			2.5
APHIS: Center for veterinary biologics			0.7
APHIS: Plant safeguarding activities	14.3	13.0	12.1
APHIS: State cooperative agreements	4.1	4.1	10.1
APHIS: Classical swine fever activities	1.0	1.7	1.0
APHIS: BSE activities	8.4	8.3	8.4
APHIS: Foot and Mouth Disease activities	9.1	9.0	9.0

Homeland Security Mission Area USDA Agency and Program	Budget authority ($ million)		
	FY2003	FY2004	FY2005 Request
APHIS: Swine feeding surveillance	4.0	4.0	4.0
APHIS: Nat'l veterinary lab - anthrax costs		0.9	0.5
APHIS: Biosurveillance			5.0
APHIS: Enhanced biosecurity		2.0	2.9
APHIS: Continuity of operations		0.2	0.2
APHIS: Security clearances		0.6	0.6
APHIS: Alkaline digester expenses	0.9	0.8	
APHIS: Wildlife services security		1.0	1.0
APHIS: Veterinary lab network		4.1	3.1
APHIS: Overseas pest risk intelligence, animal	0.7	0.7	3.0
APHIS: Overseas pest risk intelligence, plant			2.3
APHIS: Overseas surveillance, foot and mouth	0.7	0.7	0.7
OCIO: Cyber infrastructure protection	7.4	4.4	9.5
Emergency preparedness and response	**50.8**	**54.4**	**68.7**
ERS: GIS area analysis		1.0	1.0
HSS: Homeland Security Staff support		0.5	1.5
Dept. Admin.: Crisis management and planning	0.5	0.5	0.4
Dept. Admin.: Background investigations	0.5	0.5	0.5
FSIS: Office of Emergency Preparedness	2.2	2.2	2.2
FSIS: Education and training	2.3	2.5	4.5
FSIS: Technical assistance to state/local	2.2	2.2	2.2
OCIO: Training and exercises	0.1	0.1	0.1
OCIO: Planning	0.5	0.7	0.7
OCIO: Alternate interoperable communication	0.5	3.6	1.6
OCIO: Alternate facilities	0.5	0.8	0.6
CSREES: Education and training	31.6	30.8	35.8
APHIS: Emergency preparedness for states	1.0	1.0	1.0
APHIS: National Veterinary Vaccine Bank		0.3	6.6
APHIS: Other emergency management activity	8.9	7.7	10.0
Intelligence and warning	**0.8**	**0.8**	**20.0**
FSIS: Surveillance and monitoring	0.8	0.8	5.7
FSIS: Food Emergency Response Net (FERN)			10.0
FSIS: Electronic Lab Network (eLEXNET)			3.0
FSIS: Electronic compilation of lab methods			1.0
AMS: Transportation monitoring			0.3
Total	**409.9**	**325.3**	**651.0**

Source: Compiled by CRS from USDA Office of Budget and Policy Analysis spreadsheets, and Budget of the United States Government for FY2005: *Analytical Perspectives*, "Appendix: Homeland Security Mission Funding by Agency and Budget Account," [http://www.gpoaccess.gov/usbudget/fy05/pdf/ap_cd_rom/homeland.pdf].

www.ingramcontent.com/pod-product-compliance
Lightning Source LLC
Chambersburg PA
CBHW080108010626
45794CB00015B/3314